James Mark Baldwin, John Douglas Sterrett

The Power of Thought

What It Is and What It Does

James Mark Baldwin, John Douglas Sterrett

The Power of Thought
What It Is and What It Does

ISBN/EAN: 9783337812003

Printed in Europe, USA, Canada, Australia, Japan

Cover: Foto ©Thomas Meinert / pixelio.de

More available books at **www.hansebooks.com**

THE

POWER OF THOUGHT

WHAT IT IS AND WHAT IT DOES

BY

JOHN DOUGLAS STERRETT

WITH AN INTRODUCTION BY

J. MARK BALDWIN

PROFESSOR OF PSYCHOLOGY IN PRINCETON UNIVERSITY

NEW YORK

CHARLES SCRIBNER'S SONS

1896

To

MY FATHER AND MOTHER

INTRODUCTION

BY J. MARK BALDWIN

I AM glad to be able to write a few words in appreciation of the book of Mr. Sterrett; for I find it in many respects a timely and valuable work. And since my opinion is entirely professional, based on psychological reasons — for I have never known Mr. Sterrett personally — it may serve to bring the book more quickly to the notice of those who are likely to value it.

Mr. Sterrett seems to have done what many professed psychologists would like to be able to do, i.e., to write a book which interests people generally, without repelling them by scientific terms and phrases unfamiliar to the lay mind; and at the same time not to fall into that other pit of popular scientific writers, the condemnation of having cheapened science by watering it. And this general expression may serve to indicate the two merits which, to my mind, commend the present book.

In the first place, Mr. Sterrett's style is sufficiently noteworthy to draw favorable notice to his work. It is refreshingly spontaneous, unaffected, and telling; and the diction is individual and striking while not strained. For my own part, I am free to say — even though it involve a personal confession — that many of the current works on psychology seem to me in style hard, unliving, and *rein wissenschaftlich*, after reading the vivid English in which Mr. Sterrett puts his thought.

And in the second place, I find Mr. Sterrett's pages filled with points of view which are those of the latest scientific investigators. This is to me a matter of great interest; for Mr. Sterrett has written partially apart from the current of discussion. His personal semi-isolation has not impaired his results; but the rather has it heightened the effect of his personal talent, and at the same time served to give a very unusual naturalness and convincing quality to the truths which the new scientific terms and formulas make, in a measure, rigid and forbidding. I might point out such points of view in larger number; but it may suffice to signalize certain of the greater doctrines which give main purpose and character to the work.

One such point of view is that which Mr. Sterrett has embodied in his title, "The Power of Thought," and which furnishes the real motive of the whole. The doctrine that all action is the outcome of thinking, in some shape; that conduct

only reveals, and cannot help revealing, the progress of knowledge — this is now just getting to be
a doctrine of common acceptance under such terms
as " Suggestion," " Motor Elements," " Dynamogen-
esis," etc. Mr. Sterrett carries out this view in
many of its interesting bearings; among which I
find his position on the " free will " controversy
the only rational and true one. As part of this
general position, his way of stratifying consciousness, as it were, in periods, beginning with the
earliest infancy, leads him to a thoroughgoing,
genetic method which he is the first, as far as I
know, to embody in a text-book. Here again, I
think, his intuitions are, in the main, true to the
progress which genetic psychology is making.

Finally, the other thing which I would mention
about Mr. Sterrett's book is the philosophy which
he brings to it. It is dualism — the point of view
of Hamilton, and our own McCosh and Porter.
But dualism in philosophy has, heretofore, suf-
fered from an inadequate and superficial psychology. Neither the doctrine of " The Power of
Thought," nor that on which the genetic method
is founded, has been developed by the advocates
of the so-called " soul theory "; and, as a prominent psychologist has recently said, the " soul theory " needed restatement in view of the advances
of psychology in these and other lines. Quite
noteworthy is his repudiation of those traditional

burdens of dualism, the "substratum" theory and the "faculty" theory. I feel the freer in pointing out the success of Mr. Sterrett in this direction inasmuch as my own philosophical point of view is somewhat different from his. Even those who do not agree with the author, as of course I do not sometimes, will nevertheless recognize the high quality of his work.

Both in matter and form, therefore, I think Mr. Sterrett's book will be found trustworthy by the general reader, and also available by teachers in search of a text-book in the elements of psychology.

PRINCETON, July, 1896.

PREFACE

From of old, men have been much given to philosophizing. This spirit of restless inquiry is to be accounted for by the interest we all take in comprehending phenomena. The present effort is only another attempt in the same direction, differing from others, it may be, in some of its details, if not in conception. The questions treated are such as a young man may turn over in his mind, when engaged in the serious study of mental and moral problems.

The plan adopted was to write down my thoughts on any slip of paper found in my pockets, as I was walking, or riding, about the farm, or the neighborhood, and then wait, often for many days and weeks, or even months, until, after some desultory reading, or else conversation of the ordinary kind, I felt I was in a better mood to deal with some leading problem that was engaging my attention.

After some little time, I found I had a large bundle of these little slips, the which I subsequently sorted out and pinned together, as best I could. But when I undertook to compose the present monograph, I soon found that I was committed to the task of throwing away the greater number of my slips; a discovery that surprised, and discouraged, me exceedingly.

Such, in brief, is a history of the troubles I encountered when composing these pages; my first, and certainly final, attempt to address the general public. Many of the conclusions reached were by no means anticipated. Indeed, many of my former views had to be reformed, in part or whole, or else abandoned entirely, as I wrote. And the hesitation with which some friendly psychologists, to whom I handed the manuscript for an opinion, received some of my speculations, admonishes me that they will be seriously challenged. But facts and their significance must control our theories. The cold gaze of hostile criticism will reveal the truth.

In the treatment of sensations, perceptions, and conceptions, much of what I have to say is mainly expository, and in keeping with received teachings. Still, I have not felt bound to follow any authority, however eminent, reserving room for independent judgment, without encumbering the argument with any formal statement of diverging views which I could not stop to refute, in detail. The attentive reader will remark, if I mistake not, that the argument is not without an individuality of its own.

Referring now to what is said on the subjects of Environment, The Power of Thought, Emotions and Desires, Alternative Choice, The Will, etc., etc., I have to say that I am not aware of any one prosecuting these studies after the manner in which I have treated them.

And here, I would be allowed the privilege of explaining the plan I adopted for conveying my views to the reader. It will be observed that I do not offer to explain everything, at once and exhaustively, but gradually, as the reader can follow the explication. For instance, when I am considering some old problem of psychology, say the power of our thoughts, emotions, and desires, etc., I am not to be understood as bound to say, then and there, all I have to say of conation, or the will, though, as a matter of fact, that power, as will be seen in the sequel, is really as much, if not more, pronounced in these latter as in any thought considered as an intellectual energy. Each subject in hand is explained, as fully as the stage of discussion will allow of a careful approach to the more difficult points involved; an immediate explication preparing us for the heavier tasks reserved for a future page. For instance, when I am writing a sentence, I aim to put in all the qualifications needed to convey my meaning, at that time and place. I then follow up with other sentences, each of which qualifies its predecessors. And similarly, as to paragraphs, sections, chapters, and parts, as they succeed and relieve each other in orderly sequence, each and all of which are intended to qualify, and so bring out my meaning more adequately.

I acknowledge my obligations to Rev. Dr. James A. Quarles, of Washington and Lee University, Virginia, Prof. J. Mark Baldwin, of Princeton University, Prof. J. McKeen Cattell, of Columbia

College, New York, and Prof. J. R. S. Sterrett, of Amherst College, Massachusetts, for the kind interest and encouragement extended to me, under circumstances of grave anxiety and depression. For, without the assistance of these friends, this book had never seen its way to publication. In saying this, however, it is to be understood that they are not to be held responsible for anything I have written.

JOHN DOUGLAS STERRETT.

BELL'S VALLEY, VIRGINIA,
May 1, 1896.

CONTENTS

PART I

ENTERING UPON THE PROBLEM

PART II

THE ACQUISITION OF KNOWLEDGE

Part III

THE POWER OF INFORMATIONS

Part IV

PERSONAL AND VOLUNTARY POWER OF INFORMATIONS

PART I

ENTERING UPON THE PROBLEM

CHAPTER I

Preliminary Statements

I

To be a free agent, man must have the ability to achieve his freedom. Then no one but himself can be implicated in his guilt or innocence.

And therefore I shall aim in what follows to present the facts of his freedom and urge the evidence for it. If these are not to be found in his soul, then, beyond doubt, the thesis for freedom has no credible support, and we are the slaves of an unbending necessity. Man goes upon his freedom, as a valid fact consciously affirmed and never disallowed. Still there is a wide divergence of opinions when attempt is made to interpret the phenomena which either antecede or synchronize with every act of free determination.

II

Who, then, is a moral agent? How does he become such, and why responsible?

The answer to these questions may be gathered as we proceed. For the present, I take a moral agent to be a rational person placed within the play of inducements, some good, some bad, and who can prefer the one or the other, on condition, how-

ever, of personal responsibility for his choice.   An
animal has a lower and less gifted free agency.
But this is a question of comparative intellectual
vision.   Certainly man is free as to all that his
distinctive intelligence can achieve.   It remains
true, nevertheless, that man, as the unit of *all* his
powers, intellectual, animal, and moral, is free and
responsible only when he founds what he does on
conceptions of right and wrong.

The power to do right or wrong, at our option,
but with a knowledge of the inevitable consequence
that follows choice, is, therefore, what constitutes
the soul a moral factor.   For the present, however,
I can only indicate the cardinal points, in passing
— until, after some further outlining, the subject
may be studied more deliberately.

III

Here the question obtrudes itself again, How
does man become a moral agent?   I premise that
there are many things connected with what he
does for which he is not at all responsible, in the
forum of conscience.   For instance, what is purely
native and, therefore, prior to any act of his, is
not for him to account for in any way.   He comes
from a germ, and, at birth, is in no condition to
exercise the functions of a rational and moral creature, and, for long, he cannot have command of his
distinctive powers.   But we may say that he has
them in germ, or else in various stages of growth.
For the birth of adult morality is held in long
abeyance, until our rational conquests have wrought

out its deliverance fully. And the real point before
us is to determine how and when man begins to act
for himself.

Here are some facts which cannot be ignored:
We have a vital, rational, and moral capacity,
giving us, after a time, our proper personal powers.
In early infancy, these do not act with the acquired efficiency reserved for riper years.

But they take root then, and grow with the
growth of life and thought, undergoing a discursive
training which will inform us what to do, and *how*,
on experience and *judgment*.

But now when we can securely lay hands on our
ripened powers, man is set apart to enter upon a
new order of acts; namely, those which express the
force of moral convictions. He has labored up to
the position of a moral creature, and governs himself by the power of his moral conceptions. He
has entered upon a moral career; his moral freedom
is known in thought and act, because, on his discovery of moral conceptions, he has discovered a
power which he can make use of in shaping the
affairs of conscience and conduct.

IV

But whose disposition actuates him? Mani-
festly his own, if, indeed, man acquires a moral
power in acquiring moral distinctions. And yet
what is called our dispositions is vexed with an
overplus of the knottiest difficulties, most of
which, however, have their source in an order of
things coming in before our birth, and therefore

out of sympathy with the personal power acquired in amassing knowledge. The truth is, as before stated, that when one essays moral conduct, it is because he has discovered a law for right and wrong, and so *himself* evokes the awful stringency found in morals.

But, as I said, our native dispositions — even our nature and much of our environment — come in before we are born, giving each of us a peculiar individuality, even when in germ. Still, what is all this but the prelude to what is responsibly done when one is competent to command his conduct in accordance with conceptions distinctly his own? The Creator provides all this needed outfitting and antecedent furnishing, simply to have us equipped with a discursive competency to act for ourselves.

CHAPTER II

The Infant

I

THE first step in the argument for moral freedom should be an earnest and careful study of the child's mind and native forces. I am referring to its native endowments or dispositions more particularly. We are certainly governed by our dispositions, and, when acting for ourselves, must come to know them as factors which enter into our every act. However, for present purposes, let us take them to be that combination of psychical capacities, rational, animal, and moral, which opens the way to that accepted responsibility for our acts which comes of our conscious achievements.

So much, to have done with this ambiguity, for the present.

II

It may possibly aid our study to offer some explanation of how the child succeeds in acquiring the powers of a moral agent. Minute details apart, some few controlling facts may suffice for our present purposes. The child is just born. Its own life — sensations, cognitions, etc., with the concomitant emotions — comes to its apprehension on

7

first acquaintance, and as a first knowledge it knows not how or whence. It is a surprise party, without the support of even a minimum of experience to steady its unfolding powers, or to assure it of a foothold beyond its incipient struggles. It finds itself suddenly caught up into vivid consciousness from the ends of the earth, and, as yet, with no balance of judgment for confronting the unwonted powers of flesh, spirit, and nature. It wails helplessly as it makes its way into the overshadowing mystery that bangs about its ears and rings through its soul. However, thought is eager-eyed, combative, curious, and anxious for the work of interrogation and discovery, and the child becomes gradually reassured, if not aggressively active and sapient.

III

I have adverted to a few of the more obvious foundation facts found in the infant soul. And here, it is important to remember that these are vitally articulated with the supreme factors of mind and morals. And I have made mention of its struggles. At first it knows nothing, not even itself, nor thought, nor consciousness, for it has no conscious antecedents, realizing conscious thought without previous acquaintance. But in an instant, this, our child, then so inexperienced, awakens to the touch of consciousness, the hidden powers of flesh and spirit pulsing through its soul in a strange jargon. But all these beginnings of life, and thought, and action, in one so artless and inexperienced, are pregnant, supernatural facts coming direct from the Creator's mind, and there is more of the superhuman seen in them than in the more stupendous monuments of nature.

IV

I offer now a short study of the growth of the infant soul, noting some of the earlier manifestations of its powers. Prominent among these are its *native* impulses; native and therefore not to be confounded with the voluntary impulsions which are born of thought. The child has the feeling of hunger, thirst, curiosity, etc., shut up, as it is, to some vague form of unrest, or else to all the unhelpfulness and unwisdom of mere brute force. But even at that early period it can begin to energize discursively, albeit dominated by impulses, well nigh, if not altogether, animal and brutish. And therefore would I remark the more particularly how its distinctively human powers gather strength and expand in an ascending scale, as it discovers and explores the broad fields of research which invite investigation. For even such a beginner will strive to realize some of its possibilities, and act intelligently, and even responsibly, as may be presumed from the fact that, after all, the child is not an imbecile. So, at the appointed time, it will affirm knowledge and its power, and wield that power as it thinks. But when just born, it is not taught of its slumbering gifts, though their active mission will not be long delayed. Meantime, its infant wants are cared for by the mother. And as she is providing for all these, she is, at the same time, fostering the growth of its kindling intelligence.

Here a great change takes place. She informs its blind strivings, leading it afield by the light of informations addressed to its opening apperception. For though it be but a mere babe, it will soon give some first thought to what is brought to its notice. The mother is fond, and, as I said, informs her child in many tender ways. She kisses its little hurts, and it subsides into blissful, trustful, healthful, peaceful slumber. And the work of love and duty knows no intermission. The child is hers by right, divine and human, and her heart softens with blissful tenderness in its presence.

Meanwhile, it is regarding all these tactful, loving attentions with acutest, shrewdest interest. And by and by it is no longer a thing of ignorance, like a mere animal controlled by animal impulses. For, indeed, as soon as these latter are led forth in paths of human thought and achievement, they know the voice of their leader and follow him. And ever afterward, no exclusively animal, not to say brutish, impulse can determine conduct, except through some discovery of thought coming in to sanction or reject it — on condition, nevertheless, of a personal responsibility fixed upon the actor.

V

But let us define more articulately the attitude of the infant mind when touched with all these maternal ministrations.

We have seen that it is alert, attentive, and curious almost from the outset. All intelligence is active, discursive, and watchful, and the child is emotioned accordingly. For what it sees, in that first contact of its infant thought with the world of things about it, is as fascinating as a dream of perpetual spring to its heaving breast. And therefore is it the more eagerly prompted to seek knowledge and so frame some first opinions of its mother, and the form and pressure of her attentions. Effort succeeds effort, as thought succeeds thought. And so, after some brief interval, sundry modest notions will begin to crystallize in some well-grounded convictions on which to act. Still, its native animalism is not to be too hastily supplanted by the conscience and conception of its later humanity. However, we shall not wait long.

The crude native appetencies, at first so untaught, are so often directed to objects specially fitted to appease them, the child has so often traced its sensations of touch, taste, sight, etc., to what produces them, that a time comes when it can form a valid judgment upon the problem of these so urgent physical promptings and their offices; and thereupon, by reason of its now more urgent humanity, it assumes for itself the task of personally appraising, not alone sensations and their gratification, but each kind of appetency, whether native or cultivated, by its conformity or non-conformity to its judgment of what is best or preferable in view of its cultivated wants. For, indeed, all thought is a discovery, or else a clarification in order to a discovery, of something which appeals to our educated wants. And if this be so, then the child must eventually see that its every thought tends to compass the intelligent needs and broader aspirations of its now instructed humanity.

VI

As previously intimated, the first intellections of the child are not slow to present themselves. In fact, they are seen in the faintest initial glows of the dawn of consciousness, while, as yet, it cannot discern them as maturely distinct from other elements with which they are associated.

Details will be cared for, as the argument proceeds, in this and future chapters. But the point I would here make is, that the child does, finally, relieve itself from a condition of bondage to native impulsions which, as purely vital and animal, cannot be mentally defined or known at the first, as they will be through the light of discoveries that set us free from the slavery of ignorance, or feeble thinking.

For, as thought takes up its resources, the child becomes more and more under the sway of reason, though it may never, and should never, part company with what is distinctly animal and vital, lest peradventure it part company with, or at least mutilate, its characteristic humanities.

VII

I am now regarding the child as at an age when it can project a rational impulse, called emotion or desire. For thought without its power is an empty, impossible, and irrational acquisition. But there is none so feeble that it does not have at least a minimum of the power of a moral agent. Now, it is this thought, or knowledge, or conception, which furnishes the child with a *rational impulse* known as desire or emotion. But this is an anticipation.

Moreover, the child is no longer now compelled to act without thought, at the dictation of any native, or animal, impulse. The grip of thought sanctions and finalizes its acts. And what it does is done on a view of what is best for itself, judiciously, and, it may be, with many imperfections, but still with final, hearty approval. For it has now discovered within its soul the might and mystery of a dominant humanity which cannot allow the unquestioned sway of animal propensities.

It conceives a good and a bad for itself, — rational convictions fairly and honestly labored up to. It reasons, and acts with its reasons. And ever afterwards it is a rational power, governed by its own opinion of what it shall do with itself.

VIII

In due time, this infant soul makes acquaintance of still another power. Surely, but slowly, there come to it tidings of the *quality* of its own and others' actions, the good and bad, the right and wrong, of thoughts, and deeds, and actors.   In that very moment, moral power is born.   The child has conceived its first ideas of moral rectitude and depravity.   It is now a regenerated soul with power to conceive an order of acts founded on these later informations, but without the power to resume an order exclusively animal, or even simply intelligent.   It has reached the last stage of spiritual pilgrimage, and is now a moral power, versed in the law of right and wrong.

IX

I offer here a final statement of conclusions reached in this chapter.

1. At birth, the child has a body and spirit furnished of God.   These antecede its every act, being in no sense its acts, nor voluntary to it.

2. There is an ordinance of God which endows it with involuntary impulsions, or native appetencies.   These challenge recognition, and that too without dispute, until it can lay hold on its responsible powers, and so make good its ability to attemper the former by opinion and judgment. And yet, withal, though true impulses, they are not true *desires*, because, acting as *blind* instigations, they cannot be voluntary.

3. For all such original factors, going, as they do, only to an original equipment for a competent thinker, can never be lifted out of their constitutive limitations, and put to playing the part of necessity within the precincts of discursion and choice.

This would be to transmute the limitation by God's laws, and thus confound the action of heterogeneous powers — which is absurd.

4. It so happens that, just as the native impulses begin to act in the child, its thought, and subsequently its moral appreciations, rise into being, as incipient forces confronting the former. Now I am not mooting the question whether the child ever has even a single native impulse which emerges unchallenged by some qualifying mental supervision. But if so, the mind itself must have been off duty somewhere — for repairs. I am regarding the child as, once for all, equipped with rational competency, and beginning to act for itself. For, indeed, it is a power unto itself, fortified with the several resources of a far-seeing intelligence and, whenever and however acting, it is free to find its way of life by adhering to its way of thinking. As a genetic cause, belonging to the being and even anatomy of the child, necessity discharges its office once for all, but the sweep of its presence is definitely cut off by the approach of a new comer fenced in with the resources of mind, never at all acting for itself without thinking for itself.

5. Child, or, for that matter, man, has still involuntary potencies, — still everything to fit it for acting for itself. The blind impulses may still come in before its voluntary determinations, giving thus a notification of some want of the animal economy which, the child sees, requires attention in view of its own personal economy of rational wants and responsibilities.

6. The child has antecedents innumerable. It is finite. Nothing absolute about it. The reproductive agencies that made it a germ were not of its procuring. So of its nature, native endowments, involuntary impulses, etc. So, too, of the general tendency of everything around it to uphold its being and powers, of course, within the law of God which provides for its activities. So also, of heredity, idiosyncrasies, etc. All these are furnished of a creative original, in aid of the needed competency and stamp of an individual intelligence, personal and responsible. But when they have, once for all, discharged their office of ushering in, and contributing to, the being and life of the new power, they are debarred from doing anything, the doing of which is the special prerogative of that new power.

CHAPTER III

THE ADULT

I

AT that stage of our discursive pilgrimage when thought and desire have effected a mature coalescence, the child has reached manhood. Years agone, it has achieved its first ideas, and mental power is now a several cause, voluntary, personal, and decisive. A cursory view of such a power must suffice for the present.

It is the human mind conceiving, and doing, a work of its own. And such a power bids fair to discover a way to consummate its rational views. Indeed, if one were but half-witted, he could not consent to give way to any kind of act, regardless of considerations evoked on a knowledge of what is good or bad, right or wrong, for himself.

And here I may suggest a reason why we have choice in things pertaining to our conduct. It is to save the Self consciously responsible, at all hazards. For, without choice, we could never affirm ourself responsible for our acts. At all events, it is not to have the headlong push of involuntary impulses.

But we may say, it is to have charge of the power of our own thoughts, and so be responsible for our acts. And though we may do badly, by making a bad choice, yet if we are to be our own keeper, and not a crippled, irresponsible force, we must be free to choose, and do, our own acts, and so affirm a conscious, personal responsibility for both choice and acts.

II

For, if one found conduct on reasons, he cannot take a neutral position. Unbridled desires, desires misplaced, unwise, even beastly, etc., these and others, all have to be subdued to the tone and temper of the now responsible self, which will maintain the right of choice, whether it fits in with downright depravity or the clearest preceptions of duty.

Take, for example, a desire known to be immoral. Now, what shall we do? We say, we will have none of it. The desire, then, will have to take the back seat. Why? Simply because the responsible soul will have it that way.

But again, we may choose to indulge an impurity with intense preference. What say we now? I appeal to facts for answer. The same self can frame a judgment of good or bad, and choose, or side with, the bad, — and do it. Here, too, the responsible soul has its own way.

Yes, I mean it! We might have acted otherwise, but we did not, and one must have his own way, if the act is to be his and he is to be held responsible for it. The case is simply this. Man conceives his moral informations, and so affirms their obligatory character, and becomes a moral force. As such, he cannot act without choosing between good and bad, and choice fixes the responsibility upon him for his acts. He has made himself personally responsible for them.

III

It seems, then, that man is free to think, and also free to side with his thoughts, be they good or bad, but on condition of personal responsibility for choice. He acts with the efficiency of his decisive thought, and cannot refuse thus to act. He cannot abide in purely animal impulses, for he cannot withhold his rational powers in their presence. He is not a dust hole, to be filled in with the rubbish of things not his own, as a responsible creature. He is a power on earth for good or bad, or preferably for both.

He conceives a moral work, and is moved to do it, for reasons of choice; and though finite, he has, at least, more than a mere semblance of creative power, executing many works that attest the force and bent of his thoughts. He is not to be pent up in the citadel of mental and moral subjectivity. For he is both discursive and aggressive, and so what is subjectively only a thought goes out and off to its work, and labors up to a new something, quite beyond the thought as a mere conception, and gives himself a veritable creation, known as something he has done, and has done for reasons of choice. And therefore are we, in this regard, God's modifying and innovating agents at work

upon things finite, effecting, as we do, an unwonted
series of changes and consecutions among them,—
at the command, and by the power, of thought.

IV

Reverting, now, to an imperial access of power
discerning the ideas of right and wrong and the
judgment of personal responsibility which follows
its exercise, we see man rating and ranking the
deeds of himself and his familiars, by the moral
standard which he has discovered, even balancing
his conduct by conceptions of right and wrong,
as, in truth, himself alone responsible for choice
of either.

But then, he is now a moral personage begotten
of the moral conceptions he has wrought out, and
to which he must hereafter defer, just as aforetime
he deferred, more and more, to lighter and lower
considerations, as we follow him back to the less
thoughtful days of childhood. But now that he
is in the power of thought, its grip is not to be
relaxed, not even if he would.

So much in the way of general considerations.
My detailed theory will be systematically unfolded
in subsequent pages, especially when confronted
by opposing theories.

CHAPTER IV

MIND AND BRAIN

I

IN this chapter, I propose to take in hand an objection which goes to the possibility of the mind's freedom, and, if valid, closes all discussion. I refer to the theory which would trace all our acts to the "molecular changes in the brain." This is rather a question as to the origin and functions of sensations, inasmuch as it would ignore the power of mind, whilst laying stress upon that of sensation. Indeed, the argument is meant to be a sweeping denial to mind, as an efficient, constructive, discursive cause of anything. I remark, therefore, first, upon the origin of sensations. And here I may remark that they are a mode of body and brain, determined, for the most part, by something exterior to the perceiving mind. Whereas the latter, for its part, determines ideas, informations, voluntary acts, etc.

Here we see two activities in severe contrast, one of mind and one of brain, confronting each other, and interacting, at the moment of contact. The sensation is an exterior visitor to mind, and mind is not slow to give it fit welcome.

Now I had thought that we had here *two* activities interacting in severe contrast, one a mode of mind, and the other a mode of body! It seemed, therefore, bluntly plain that as each acted from its own centre, so each had a power distinctly its own. But now that I find scientists affirming that as every act of mind has a material antecedent in the brain, such act is, for that reason, a *material result*, I must confess to a mild surprise.

We meet with the following from Du Bois-Reymond: "We are accumulating the proof that consciousness is bound to material antecedents. The condition of a whole world, even of a human brain, at each instant, is the absolute *mechanical* RESULT of the condition in the previous instant, *and* the absolute *mechanical* CAUSE of the condition in the following instant."

Here, we have both cause and result affirmed to be mechanical, and consciousness bound to both material factors. For it is explicitly stated that a condition of brain at each instant is a mechanical *result*, and that this result is the absolute mechanical *cause* of its subsequent condition, and that consciousness is bound to these mechanical conditions.

I am a novice in all this grand, rhetorical disputation, but I must confess to some little knowledge of consciousness, and what it affirms. And I am at a loss to divine a plausible excuse for such a palpable perversion of the facts of psychology. Its absurdity will be apparent when we begin to realize the controlling fact that the mechanism of the material universe, as well as that of the brain,

" is bound to " a law of God which prescribes and
circumscribes, and so allows for the action of both
mind and brain, a condition for both, such that
brain is as much " bound to " an immaterial cause,
as the latter is bound to the mechanics of brain.
Now, because one set of actions is mechanical is
no reason why another set should also be mechanical. Because a kite sails by mechanical forces is
no reason why it should not be held in check by
a voluntary effort on the part of the kite-holder.
Each should have the benefit of its diversely
attempered powers.

I do not object to brain having all its thronging,
mechanical transformations, and, for that matter,
many more. Let us have them all. For mind
could never, at all, be a power unto itself without
some way of coming to a knowledge of exterior
powers, and acting upon that knowledge. On the
other hand, it is just as certain that brain could
never have, at any " instant," a single one of its
vital or physical, otherwise mechanical, causes and
results, if mind were off duty, or, in some other
way, out of place.

The two must stand or fall together. No mind,
no physical sensations! No physical sensations,
no mind, because no object for its discursive activities! But more of this in succeeding paragraphs!

Before proceeding further, I may explain that,
if the author could be understood to mean that
mind and brain are united in one organism whose
phenomena are conjunct, dependent, and concur-
rent, I should not controvert that view, allowance

being made for the plain limitations to the action of both.

For I admit that the two are mated at birth, and grow up together, one maturing mental, as the other matures nervous, or physical, potencies. But I protest against the intimation that this union secures only material causes and results.

The truth is that both mind and brain are finite, and, therefore, restricted and controlled, each by its conditions and rôle of action; each existing, and acting its part, by, and because of, the enabling laws which, whilst prescribing what is peculiar to each, confine each to its prescribed mode of being and activities. The function of each is held to the most inviolable restrictions, and if so held, it is needless to say that neither can transcend the sweep of its powers.

But retiring Du Bois-Reymond for a season, let us reinforce him by another great scientist. Says Tyndall: "We believe that every thought, and every feeling, has its definite mechanical equivalent; that it is accompanied by a certain breaking up and remodelling of the atoms of the brain," etc. This is much like Du Bois-Reymond's argument. Both seem to argue from the mechanics of brain to mechanics of mind.

Still one should be thankful that Tyndall seemingly permits thought to accompany, and perhaps finger, the all-embracing mechanics somewhat vaguely, being "accompanied by a certain breaking up, and remodelling of the atoms of the brain," though, it may be, only as a spectator. And for

my part, I am far from denying that mind and
brain may work together in prescribed and restricted
relations, but I am as far from admitting that this
working together of mind and brain, as far as it
goes, turns up only mechanical causes and results
for what mind does.

May I inquire, does this admitted coördination
of the two powers contravene the functional prerogatives of either, in the slightest particular?
What if the whole effect of such a close union of
the two is to conserve, and uphold, the several
dissimilarities allotted to each, in its appointed
sphere of action! One cannot act without the other,
or for that matter, be what it is, simply because of
a pre-arrangement for a restricted dual action, and
appointed results. And so, if there be a union of
two activities, such as that of mind and brain, in
order to conjoint results, no one need be surprised
that the functions of each will disclose points of
dependence on that union, disclosing features, let
us imagine, widely different from what they would
be, if each could act in disunited severalty. Moreover, I shall treat them, as I find them, compacted
together, "one and inseparable" — through life.
But will an arrangement that secures the connected, finite, and, therefore, restricted, actions
of mind and brain, obliterate the characteristic
functions of either? Will the action of brain
make that of mind all material, or that of mind
make that of brain all immaterial? Still, one supposition is quite as reasonable as the other, and
both are lamentably incredible. And if so, what

becomes of all this twaddle of scientists about the absolutely mechanical causes and results of brain upon mind?

II

Suppose, now, that we wish to have a discursive but *free* activity hold communion with things material and physical, and set up a power distinctly its own, even the power of knowledge, in their midst, and with that view put mind and body together in one organism, and thus succeed in securing our object!

Here, we are in need of some explanations, more philosophical than psychological.

It is evident that mind cannot be mind, unless it gets knowledges, and it cannot get these except the object of knowledge be placed within its reach. Hence the need for that intimate union of mind and brain which brings them into immediate contact, and by which the former can take instant cognition of the latter, and in this way, have some proximate object within its reach, on which it can act discursively. Now, it is by this very device, that mind, in respect of the physical sensations presented in the sensorium, has its sole possible opportunity, under the fundamental laws which prevail herein, to perceive, or reason, and ultimately know and do many things. Think of an act of cognition! A sensation, being a mode of brain, swims into the mind's presence, giving the latter an opportunity instantly to lay hold of an object lodged in the sensorium — an object which it would by no means know, if mind and brain could not come into the immediate presence of each other. And herein lies the ultimate justification for the intimate compacting of the two factors concerned, the direct contact of the perceiving mind with outer objects giving it a firmer grasp upon powers not its own, even those of matter, and its inner and outer correlations.

And here I could wish to give my views more clearly.

I maintain that, when matter and spirit are bound together in an organism, at once vital, animal, and thoughtful, there will emerge a series of interactions so dependent on that union, that a given change will disclose a voluntary result, let the coöperating mechanics of the brain be what it may.

And, therefore, I insist that, if the social compacting of two such factors as mind and brain, allows of certain limited interactions between the two, I am unable to divine why such compacting of the two should result in either one swallowing up the peculiar causal efficiency of the other. Is the centre for discursive causation so infringed upon that it cannot contribute its own efficiency? Does organization of two powers mean the conservation of one, and the annihilation of the other?

Can any good reason be assigned for this mutilation of the dualism of mind and brain? If not, how can we hold that the antecedent condition of brain furnishes "the absolute *mechanical* cause" of any condition of mind, in *any* instant? What becomes of mind and its cognitive powers working along with, and upon, every mechanical antecedent that can pretend to be a cause in contact, and in contrast, with the former?

I was assuming that the two were mated together for a conjoint work which required the active intervention of their diverse efficiencies. But here, we are startled with the *scientific* discovery (?) that brain engineers its work so successfully, that it utterly displaces the causal efficiency of its co-worker! The thing is abundantly unthinkable. Brain can be a material cause, though "bound to" mind, but mind cannot be an immaterial cause, because "bound to" brain!

And yet, this is what *science* teaches. However, one could take it better, if these advanced thinkers would only condescend to explain why mind should not have the credit of its powers as distinctly and cheerfully affirmed, as they affirm those of brain.

III

A few plain statements will vindicate a truer science without belittling either mind or brain. Mind is the ideating centre, and whatever else brain may do, it cannot deliver *one single idea*. Its data are intra-cerebral excitations, called sensations, and it delivers these, and these only. *Per contra*, mind, for its part, begins a work of thought on these physical deliverances of the co-working brain. It acts promptly, in order to the power of knowledge.

It *perceives* these physical or cranial excitations and, therefore, undertakes to remark upon their peculiarities and outlying affiliations, what they are, and what they do, why they impinge conscious- ness, the hence and wherefore of their mission, what their significant traits or qualities, and so acquires some important informations, and frames some opinions, of these exterior potencies, and connects all this knowledge with its conscious intelligent, or vital wants.

Apparently, Tyndall allows somewhat for this power of mind, though I am not too sure of this. With him, as it appears to me, thought has some semblance of power to remodel the atoms of the brain. But if that is all it can do, it might as well be cast out entirely. For it is preëminently a con- scious, aggressive, constructive, causative potency, discovering and utilizing power with every dis- covery of knowledge, and building up a rational and moral government of its own, in conscious contrast with material or physical causes.

As intimated, I may not do exact justice to Tyndall. Perhaps, perhaps! But the candid admission that thought has some power to remodel the atoms of the brain would be a very damaging argument against the position of Du Bois-Rey- mond, who compromises both the spirituality and freedom of the mind.

IV

But to continue our analysis.

In a spirit of conciliation, we may, for the nonce, defer to the contention of scientists, by supposing that the spirituality and immateriality, if not free-

dom, of the mind may be imperilled by its connection with the brain. If that is the difficulty, let us
agree to have the connection absolutely severed.
Here we light upon the *animus* of all this scientific
splutter about the material antecedents of mind.
Our Creator would have our freedom but *finite*,
connecting it with a physical body, and unnumbered other conditions, and straightway a cry is
made about the power of sensations, nerves, brain,
atoms, etc.

Now, is there any warrant in reason for this
scientific ululation? Will scientists have finite
thought, or, for that matter, anything finite, without finite limitations? Is their idea of freedom
such as to require absolute and unconditioned
powers? The whole material creation is finite,
bound, hand and foot, by fixed limitations, and
never the feeblest wail from any scientist! And
is it so astonishing to find that our thinking
faculty, also, has to walk by a law of discursion
which limits its action?

It is even so. Our thinking substance has to
walk by a law which confines, and conditions, its
activities. Nevertheless, have we any right to
complain of restrictive conditions which do but
provide a way for the play of our rational activities? Let us rather be thankful that all our possibilities are surrounded by such safeguards.

That men of science should resort to such
arguments from what brain does, as a proof of the
mechanics of mind, is a sign of the times. What
can be the motive? If you could annihilate matter,

they would stumble on another batch of affectations. They would see to it that thought should be compromised in some way. They would cry out: "The condition of a human intellect, at each instant, is the absolute intellectual *result* of its condition in the *previous* instant," complaining, thus, that all our mental procedures are determined by the state of mind in the previous instant, and not by the proper freedom of the present — and so are determined *necessarily*.

But, in all seriousness, is there any reason for staggering thought at a creative act which provides for the interdependence and co-action of brain and free discursion? We depend on God for every structural or constitutive factor which enables us to act, and which, so far from upsetting the power of thought to determine acts for which we are responsible, is His method for establishing that power. And if so be we can think and act under this dual arrangement, this is a sufficient vindication of our rational, and voluntary, procedures.

Then, why should not the work of thought go on, under the conditions and stipulations of the original ordinance? We never hear of scientists looking out for some original crookedness, in that brain is bound to an *immaterial* cause and result. And yet, brain is as much conditioned by thought, as thought by brain. Where is the difficulty in God's creating, and upholding, a being who can think, and act, discursively under conditions which enable him to assert his unique powers, in contrast and correlation with other powers not mental?

All this to repel the intimation that the mechanics and molecules of the brain determine our acts, or else, that mind is so under duress to brain that it may be either quietly ignored, and belittled, or else, contemptuously dismissed, as an irrelevant quantity.

V

On supposition of the absolute severance of mind and brain, how could the former affirm anything exterior? On the other hand, how could brain deliver sensations within reach of a mental power out of all connection with it? But their union in one organism, such as we have it in man, provides a way for the accepted interactions of both. It is through their organic union that mind enters upon its appointed mission of discovering that which is denied to brain,— voluntary impulsions, rational satisfactions, and the joy and triumph of free determinations. And in discovering all these, it is discovering powers consciously its own, and re-affirmed in their continual employment.

But again, in case of an absolute severance of the two, knowledge would depend so entirely on an original ability to *receive* it, that the mind could scarcely be regarded as an active party to its acquisition. Query! Would this almost altogether receptive condition of mind leave man responsible? Knowing truth through a capacity for receptive appropriation, it could never be ours by the accepted processes of active exploration and discovery. We could not, then, be held responsible for thoughts, or opinions, which were not acquired by a searching study of observed phenomena. An arrangement for formulating all knowledge without effort on our part would contract our personal responsibility immeasurably.

VI

Recalling now Tyndall's words that "the brain molecules can move only in a determined way," I venture some further remarks.

We may allow all this, when truthfully explicated. His proposition has been so stated, however, as to provoke the inference that rational acts can have no rational antecedents, because the "molecules of the brain can move only in a determined way." This I demur to for the following reasons, among others reserved for a future page: That brain should have its appointed way of action is no reason why mind should not have its appointed way of action, or, for that matter, co-action. If the one is privileged to move mechanically, why not the other, to move rationally? Neither can at all move save as it conforms to the law for their interaction. It is here that the fundamental error of scientists emerges — from Darwin downwards. They make natural selection, environment, etc., preach the gospel of mechanics everywhere in the universe, allowing nothing for inborn, original, and ineradicable distinctions, which can never be mistaken for, or confounded with, the preachments of natural selection, environment, etc. In any serious discussion of the interactions of mind and brain,

D

whilst claiming those of brain to be mechanical, we should with equal candor, and better science, concede those of mind to be discursive and voluntary — even rational and selective.

For my part, I concede a thorough-going coördination and dependence of mind and brain, thought and sensor organs, both in order to any power of brain and in order to any power of mind, in respect of the perception and elaboration of phenomena of the former. For what brain does can never be recognized as a presence, can never be studied and known, except by some intelligence.

VII

Coming now to a final view of the interaction of mind and brain, I propose to inquire if the combination of the two in man makes him an automaton? If so, his acts should disclose that fact. Now, the one true and decisive way of testing this is to ascertain the nature and character of his mental powers and acts, gathering up what is distinctive and setting it over against the physical or mechanical transformations of brain.

If when subjected to this test, it is seen that thought and its efficiencies have nothing material in them; if the soul acts as it reasons, and can never in any way act without some sufficient reason for so acting; if when mated with brain, and because so mated, it comes in contact with phenomena which it rates as physical and material, knowing that they are not its own conscious powers and activities, then in possessing these peculiar traits, and in affirming this conscious knowledge of phenomena not its own, it swings off from matter as a wholly distinct energy, certifying the attributes of an immaterial essence. And whilst this view conserves both sensation and thought, it proclaims also the fact of the intercommunion of diverse powers departing from diverse centres.

Finally, I insist that mind and brain were put together for a conjoint work, each contributing its appointed portion, according to its several ability. Still, all depends on the character of the union. The law for its destined work is with the original ordinance, even as what is impossible to it is, with some disabling inhibition, found in the same ordinance; yea, more, ere it can act at all, its possibilities are irreversibly determined.

I repeat! Brain can deliver a sensation, with prompt, unerring certitude, but never an idea. It is an exciting cause to discursion, but never the causal efficiency released by a thought or idea; and what it does is in order to what the latter does. It conditions thought, opening the way to an assertion of a constructive or final power born with the thought, just as the latter conditions the delivery of sensations, giving them that discursive appreciation, without which they can have neither mission, nor existence even. But much of this is an anticipation of what will be further brought out in succeeding connections.

CHAPTER V

ENVIRONMENT

CLOSELY connected with the discussions of the previous chapter is the more general one of *Environment*, or the power of our surroundings.

I

Our first problem is to determine what Environment is. Speaking in general terms, it is everything that conditions, or limits, our personal powers. For example, whatever is exterior to a present thought has a power exterior to that thought, and so may condition it. This embraces, in particular, all the bodily organs and mental capacities born with us; as also, native propensities, sensations of the external; all our former thoughts, heredity, the abounding world without, and the progressive development of every power that gives us an enlightened hold on our distinctively human resources, enabling us to set up a new order of environment due to some dominant power of our thought. What comes through heredity, what through an original endowment of organs, etc., what through previous thoughts, and their order of progressive achievement, so far as these impress a present attitude of thought, is a very proximate, and ever-present, environment, or qualifying limitation. What comes from the outer world is an ultra, or remote, environment. But they all conspire to clear the way for the innovating powers of mind. Such in conception is environment.

II

I have already indicated briefly how these outside forces transmit impressions within reach of the mind's apperception, not omitting mention of some of the paths along which they travel. My hasty, preliminary exposition makes it plain that matter delivers up to cognition the whole body of sensations through the sensor organs, and, also, that this delivery would be void of its particular kind of result, if mind did not perceive and appraise its contents. For if mind were not actively present and studiously appreciative, there could be neither percept, nor concept, without whose intervention an exterior potency were utterly unable to place a sensorial perturbation within the pale of its jurisdiction. A sensation is but a physical impression in the sensorium, not an idea, not knowledge, not consciousness. It acts in virtue of a law which cries halt to its presenting anything at all like the latter. And, *vice versa*, the same despot cries halt to the latter's presenting a sensation, save when it mediates a share in producing a sensorial impression, as in vision, deglutition, etc., when we voluntarily employ our members in ministering to the wants of nature, or life, etc.

The old problem of the interaction of sensations

and thought, is here, as ever, only a question of the power of environment, as seen in its sensorial manifestations and the discursive power which undertakes to know of their mission.

III

You remark that we have allowed for the fact that external impressions reach the sensorium, for the most part, without our direct intervention. And now, I am referring to them, in order to bring out the point, as often urged, that the normal pressure of an exterior power either antagonizes, or else displaces, the power of discursion and choice. Now, I am not denying that ordinarily such a power does act on us without our procurement, exercising, as it does, a pressure just sufficient to awaken the slumbering activities of mind. This is, however, but a helpful service of a neighboring, and co-active, potency, coming in to put us to our own resources, affording thus an opportunity for a display of the facts, and feats, of mind.

Free powers, though finite and limited, are, nevertheless, free within their limits, just as other powers are limited by a law for their diverse reactions. And no power can displace a power not its own in kind. But free or not free, it is what it is by the fundamental law which prescribes the co-acting and co-terminous limitations to the two. And, therefore, if the point and pinch of an exterior pressure leave us still self-centred, active, and rational, it may have discharged an office of great importance for us, without ever violating any prerogative of thought found within its prescribed limitations. For our claim to discursive freedom founds upon, and within, the scope of our powers, as thus circumscribed, and not beyond that scope. It stands upon what is consciously a work of conscious power, that is to say, an achievement of our thought, opinion, information, judgment, or knowledge, and the power that is born with these. Observe, further, that all this trumped-up constraint of environment, at least as far as it may be looked upon as an intruder and outsider, comes in before the free power takes up its counter-weapons, and thinks and acts for itself. How, then, can the former contravene the action of a correlative power that does not propose to act for itself until it is in the presence of something upon which it can act? Let the former impact the latter ever so forcibly, this latter will still be free to take action, within normal limits, unless wholly upset. The plain truth is that, so far as things exterior can act on us, they do but furnish conditions, or limitations, such as subserve our mental and moral economy. Being themselves finite, and, therefore, restricted to special transformations of their own which they deliver within reach of the mind's power, they can never nullify that all-comprehending law for the interaction of diverse entities which compels a deference to all other entities with which they are associated. And the reciprocity applies equally to the one and the other, exterior things furnishing what we cannot, because we are shut up to what actions are our own, whereas we furnish what is not theirs, because they are shut up to their own.

This is, however, but an averment that, by an ordinance of Heaven, we are estopped by barriers which confine us, as all else, to our, and their, delegated powers. We are not free, save as we are restricted by the safeguards placed within our nature, or else defined by our external conditions.

I insist, therefore, that, so far as a material entity performs the office of presenting objects within the reach of mind, it simply remits us to acts of conscious intelligence. For, when such an exterior cause is freely interviewed by the intelligence, the latter begins its proper work of acquiring knowledge, discovering ideas, such as those of an exterior thing and its attributes, existential, or else dynamic; actors and actions, and what they import to us, relations and finite limitations, subjective and objective powers; and what to do with them as neighboring factors co-acting with itself, etc.

For I maintain that, when an outer force does but afford an opportunity for the conceptive and reconstructive efforts of mind, it cannot touch the latter with any, the faintest, trace of constraint; such an impossible constraint being nothing, in this regard, but a co-acting and subsidiary force presenting its meaning and mission, in its appointed way, and with proper sensorial emphasis, to the court of reason.

I conclude, then, that thought has its initiative and rôle of action through its conditions, inner and outer, ever coming to a knowledge of both, and so developing powers of its own in the careful study of what the one and the other is and does, in order to what it can do with them, in view of its own possibilities. And yet in order to any knowledge of powers within its reach it has to defer to the fundamental laws for affirming the facts, and so enlisting the powers of environment. It must go over the objects of knowledge, and make out the distinctions of an egoistical subject and an exterior object, remarking the powers, qualities, etc., of each.

IV

So far, I have been considering the power of environment, inner and outer. I turn, now, to that of mind. Its attitude toward sensations, and animal appetites, how it made the acquaintance of its subjective environment, and laid hold upon its personal wants, and what would satisfy them, — all this has been briefly adverted to, as the argument progressed. This great problem it succeeded in solving, and then set out along the path to remoter and wider discoveries. It remains, now, to follow this inquisitive, restless *person*, as he makes his way out of himself into the regions beyond, and becomes, more and more, individual, personal, and human.

He is a master spirit on the floor of the finite. As he makes progress by conscious and designed efforts, he is but keeping pace with the sequences of his thoughts. He does not part company with his environment, of whatever kind it may be, but keeps within the law for the interaction of thought and the powers which condition its exercise. He can react on his environment, and constrain it to serve his purposes to an extent limited only by the grasp of his conceptions. And, so far as he can relieve himself from the despotism of its blind forces (for it would be a remorseless despotism, if he could not affirm some power of thought to combat it), and act upon his knowledge, he is a law-giver unto himself, putting the force of his thought into his laws.

And what we say of man applies to all animals, as far down as thought is a power in them, each and all modifying his environment, as each has power of mind to do it. And, therefore, would I affirm the irresistible conclusion that we are free, only as we can lay hold of power to lead out the forces of nature, and give them unwonted extension, — even an unwonted environment, — modifying her to the extent of the rational valuations made in aid of our cultivated wants.

For it is in this way that mind, as conditioned, or even constrained, by what is not itself (and what is not thus constrained by the fundamental laws of being?), acquires power to elicit facts, and resolving them into their logical and dynamical applications, connects this latter knowledge with our welfare, and so conditions the very things by which it is itself conditioned.

But all this is in virtue of a law which, whilst it constrains thought to prescribed limits and functions, enables it to enter upon the latter, as a discursive energy freely modifying, or else educing, the powers of things exterior.

With such a system of laws prevailing in the universe of matter and mind, and obvious to our contemplation, we may avail ourselves of their sanction, study their import, and extend their application to human interests. And we may do this, not simply from what we see of external nature, but because we have a penetrating insight into our own powers, and can act up to our insight.

V

We have just seen that matter and spirit are held fast to their limited spheres of action, each conforming to a law which limits it to special functions. I mention further some other controlling facts.

Every entity must act within the measure of its competency. And none can hold itself aloof from powers with which it must associate. An inviolable law for their interaction governs both the one and the other, exacting the most undeviating reciprocity of intercourse. In other words, each has its appointed way of acting, in deference to the appointed ways of the communicating brotherhood of entities.

For indeed, the way provided for a finite thing to act had to be conceived from the beginning by appointing a mode of interaction for a universe of things socially coördinated. And here, we are evoking that fundamental law of universal creation to which all things finite must conform. For everything, be it matter or spirit, is subordinated to the enabling laws which condition its existence and determine the sweep of its powers, compelling it, willy-nilly, to slip into the traces of the finite, under pain of a merciless extinction. If, then, thought is thus tensely conditioned, and therefore finite, both by the law for its special work, and that for the action of exterior entities, so, also, is matter, both by the law for its special work, and that for its commerce with discursive entities.

It follows, therefore, that when things are put together, under a law for reciprocal co-action, they cannot act *contra*-socially. Hence, also, certain forces are called forth which express this feature of social intercourse. Moreover, what is finite cannot act as an outlaw, and so put at naught an all-embracing law of creation. For, as just now intimated, it can have command of its own special law of action, only by keeping within the scope of that wider law for interaction by virtue of which its own powers are unalterably apportioned and conditioned. And, therefore, may we say of our thought that it cannot break up any natural power, in order to its discursive work.

Whenever it would essay any preconcerted work, it never runs counter to any law of nature. And the latter provides conditions, limitations, opportunities, co-acting forces; furnishes, in fact, if not another, but non-conscious, intelligence, at least, a monumental record of creative thought, for communion with ours. For a law of nature is a thought of nature's God fixed in His work, an evidence of a superhuman mind, imperishable, and indisputable.

VI

I may now append some general observations.

It seems, then, that mind is a distinct immaterial essence, fledged with discursive competencies distinctly individual, though mated with body, and in spite of innumerable powers which act upon it, from within and from without, and on which it must depend for a hold on its own resources.

Yea, more, I contend that, if you take away a single one of these co-acting familiars, you may so disrupt its original constitution that, in default of objects presented to its initial apprehension, and their ready and powerful coöperation, you would have little to apprehend primarily, and consequently, few, if any, objects for thought, and no power to conceive any. And so you could neither reason nor act, having nothing before you for thought or action, not one working efficient for proclaiming the soul immortal, or immaterial, or indeed making proclamation of anything, unless perchance knowledge should seek us out, and get itself pasted in our pate by some unimaginable process.

I confess, though, that some of us are made painfully aware of our limitations and the power of our environment. We compare ourselves with our acquaintances, and take sorrow for our not having a better showing of mental power for our work upon the things that environ us. Yet, even we are well satisfied to have the soul furnished of God with His number of preëxisting and coëtaneous

conditions and finite limitations; yes, satisfied to
have mind and brain so put together that there will
be a well-established concomitance between a physical object acting within the brain and the counter-
action of conception and judgment within the mind,
— the brain mediating molecular and mechanical
excitations; the mind, ideas, volitions, deeds, etc.,
etc.

Distinctions reserved for the next chapter will
give all needed qualification of previous statements.

CHAPTER VI

Thought a Free Single

I

THIS chapter is an anticipation of the main facts that enter into the succeeding ones. I propose, however, to offer some thoughts which, lying within the scope of the general subject, may be advanced in connection with the preceding discussions.

But now I wish to inquire briefly, how thought is, or becomes, a free single.

I remark, first, that things are single, by reason of distinctive characters of their own. Indeed, what is void of such characters is emptied of every feature of existence. It must have either material or immaterial constituents to avouch a nature peculiar to itself, as well as divergent from other entities. The tiniest molecule of the most impalpable gas has its full complement of characteristic elements, features, attributes, etc., to give it distinguishing individuality. Lacking these, it is *nil*.

Now, in this regard, and for the same reasons, thought is set apart from all other things by an appointed variety of uniquely significant attributes. It is hence a *free* single, by virtue of specific traits, which forbid its confounding with other things. For what is conception and responsible choice can never be commuted into material consecutions and transformations. The inhibition is absolute and thoroughgoing. Thought is a free single.

II

I pass, now, to a point which concerns the first contact of thought with sensations.

As already adverted to, we have a nervous system which subserves mental functions through the sensations which it presents to mind, primarily as without significance, until mind has mediated their import.

As such, they are the first exterior objects held up before mind for its apprehension.

I am careful to note that these sensations (though at the first, they may not be full clearly differentiated by their characteristic marks) are but the means to the peculiar procedures of thought, their special office being that of bringing up the latter to its birth, and the assumption of its intellectual prerogatives.

But, now that we have thought thus aroused into a state of conscious intelligence and wakefulness, we should bear in mind that it is not a being · of sensations only, and conscious only of these. It is more. For it has a being and activities of its own, as individual as any set of distinctive characters can insulate one thing from another.

We are now considering sensations in order to their contrast with the conscious intelligence that perceives them.

As modes of body, they are as truly outer to the

mind as the flow of the blood, or the growth of the hair, the only difference being that one is conceived sooner than the other exteriority. As such modes, they all come within reach of some power of mind, and so when the latter takes them in hand, we have to witness another power at work, an energy that gives us a different result. For, in order to our having any physical phenomena reported by and held in mind, we must needs transform them into cognitions or psychical achievements. And, therefore, may we say that what makes a sensation a mode of body is a physical organism, and what cuts it away from the physics of brain or body is a mental organism with cognitive powers of its own. But when once a fact of mind, it is no longer a cerebral sensation. It is a spent sensorial excitation, and cannot be reconstructed — unless, indeed, we induce its repetition experimentally.

Now, if I am right in these speculations, the child, shortly after birth, has many sensations, intellections, and emotions confronting each other, and interacting as diverse factors. The result is the pronounced first steppings of thought. It *perceives* the sensation, and, so, acquires an *idea* of it, in response to the sensorial impression. But this response is only an affirmation of the existence of an exterior disturbance; for mere perception affirms only the existence of an object, as hereinafter to be explained.

But this is an act of mind setting out with the first appearance of sensation, giving it some cognitive attention. Here, an illustration of this diver-

E

sity, and severalty, of mind and sensation, may be
profitably pondered. The latter is to the former
what the earth is to our power of locomotion. We
can by no means take a step without a support to
our feet. Still, the ground, as a pedestrian plat-
form, is altogether dissimilar to locomotion on its
surface.

III

The requirements of the problem impel us to
notice a much wider diversity between a sensation,
and, say, an induction, as a distinctive achievement
of a free, and several, energy.

A sensation, if only perceived, is but an observed
fact discovered in the animal sensorium. Whereas,
a conception is the tension of the teleological reason
upon a sensorial perturbation, in order to that
broader knowledge of what can be affirmed of its
bearing on our personal welfare.

Let me illustrate this, also.

If a grain of wheat die, it is replaced by a
similar grain. But, if a sensation die, it is not replaced by another sensation. Something wholly
different is turned up, namely, either a simple idea,
as in perception, or else, some conviction or conception that is constructive of the strictly human
wants caught up from wider rational processes.
And, herein again, thought is seen to be a free
single. As an excitation in the sensorium, a sensation is, I repeat, an object upon which thought can
rest, but when simply perceived it arrests attention, only to its presence, *in loco;* and, thereupon,

thought initiates, after its own way, that metamorphic scrutiny which certifies the marks and rational
make-up of the things interviewed, and how they
can be availed of, as discoveries interwoven with
the discovery of our responsible interests.

Whereupon, as soon as a sensation discharges
its office, it is displaced by a different factor.
And forasmuch as this latter is a consciously intelligent energy, it will proceed to acts of conception and volition had in conscious contrast
with acts not its own, whether sensational or
not.

I am explaining mind by the marks that give
it an individuality of its own, as seen when battling with, or else making use of, forces found in
the field of environment, inner and outer.

If we were only conscious, all we could know
would be that modification of the brain, called a
sensation, and consequently, all we could do
would be to observe, without discrimination, such
phenomena as find their way into the sensorium.
Moreover, if we could not acquire those aforementioned constructive informations which go to
build up and conserve our educated requirements,
such meagre knowledge as that of a mere sensation, consciously, but witlessly, affirmed, would
stand, it may be at the threshold of, but certainly,
exterior to, the precincts of the logical understanding.   It is to be remarked that I am stating
nothing but the child's, or, for that matter, man's
honest outlook in the presence of sensations,
whose more simple elements, such an one may

not, at any time and for any reason, be able to discover.

Indeed, to be conscious only of what transpires in the sensorium is to be like one who, having had no previous experience of sonorous vibrations, becomes suddenly aware of some fine music played for his benefit. The sonorous visitation is certainly very uncanny. Something so undefined is poking at him such a storm of bewildering fuss! His apperceptions are set ajar by the crankiest emotions of surprise, fear, and wonder at the anomalous intrusion! What is that music to him in such a state of perplexity and pale affright? Is it some rude decussation of the auditory nerves? Or, is it an irruption of ill-boding monsters from the regions beyond? Or, again, will he take it as an undifferentiated sound, a mere noise, or thud? The situation is enigmatical. However, the rational centre will in due time succeed in resolving all these enigmas of sensation into conceptions vitally connected with our maturing wants and educed susceptibilities.

Wherefore, in reliance upon the foregoing statements, I submit that we have some facts placed beyond controversy. We have an exterior power working upon the sensorial centre and landing there an impression called a sensation, but, nevertheless, on condition of another power with unconfounding functions of its own going forward to meet this exterior power, giving it vogue, as a sensorial individuality contrasting with the cognitive power. But this latter power, because of

its conscious intelligence, undertakes to interpret and publish what the exterior one is, and
does; acquiring, in time, the power to transform a purely physical excitation in the sensorium into the transcendent facts and acts of a
voluntary and responsible actor.

Now, herein, again, we have the stamp and mark
of a free single with voluntary resources of its own,
in contrast with one which it affirms to be exterior
and involuntary.

IV

But, if thought be a single entity, is it voluntary?
Can it surmount the mechanics of the brain and
act on achievements of its own? And how?
These questions will receive a hurried passing
notice, in order to prevent our misconceiving its
nature or functions.

For, if mind is but a big pocket for storing away
the raw materials of sensation; if to know blue,
we have to take the pigment of the sky and stuff
it bodily within the centre of cognition; if we have
to clutch sound and tumble it about in the audito-
rium; if the rose, itself, has to be felt within the
soul, instead of being æsthetically affirmed and
appreciated; if it takes this to give us a knowledge
of personal (emotional and voluntary) power to determine our acts,—then we can never, at all, get it.

But, if, by divine appointment, we can act cognitively on exterior things, when they are acting
dynamically on our sensor organs; if to know
them is to make their acquaintance and make up

our mind what to do with them, and what to do with ourselves; that is to say, if knowledge is the appropriation and appreciation of some facts, plus a judgment of what we shall do with them, then, we can know, and do even as we know. For indeed, we can know nothing of anything, save as thought gains power to discover the rational evidences that betray what it is, and to certify them as finds seen to be promotive of our responsible ends.

Now, I claim for thought that, from the very beginning, it has to discover and appropriate all the informations on which it acts, and that it acts on the force of the reasons acquired in the exercise of its cognitive, and logical, resources, and that, if it has to acquire these informations in order to power over its own acts, it is a free and several unit, with power to propound a work exact to the thoughts that determine it; the result being that, when brain brings a physical irritation (here sensation) within reach of the mind's explorative purview, the latter can, in turn, set to work upon that object, and achieve what is denied to the former; namely, thoughts, revelations of discursive power, etc.

And here, again, I repeat, we have the same old entities confronting each other, with powers peculiar to each, one material, the other immaterial and free by a divine right to its own discoveries.

V

I continue our analysis in order to bring up some other aspects of the problem. I have remarked upon the success of thought in capturing informations. But after all, what will it do with them, and wherefore do? The explanation is evident. If it has been at pains to acquire knowledges, it will be at pains to discover what to do with them. It will see a reason for taking advantage of all it knows.

Here, then, we have a discursive entity which, when about to enter upon a given work, must study the conditions of the problem : what is a furtherance, and what a hindrance ; what is to be the effect on itself and other things when the act is done, and what deliberate conclusion will finally determine choice and personal responsibility for an act that may, or may not, be done. For its acts are determined by reasons, and, if so, it is a free cause, and as distinctly individual as significant traits can make it.

And here, we may not overlook, in passing, the marked feature of interest thought takes in its own ways and work, not seldom contrasting itself, as an aggressive and responsible energy, with things not itself. We have many facts like the following: What are our powers in the presence of all these sensational exteriorities, or, else, how shall we lead out, or otherwise evade, the forces of nature, when hostile? But these are questions for an immaterial, constructive, individual, and personal energy. And, if it can propound such questions, or for that matter, any question, it is not only free, but, in affirming such powers and prerogatives, in contrast with others which it would control, or combat, it is, in fact, affirming itself a free single. For, such a propounder must know that he has powers of his own, and that he can develop, out of his own resources, a plan, or concept, of work which he can accomplish.

And, here again, we have plan, deliberation, nerve, personal interest, self-command, and executive ability, — the very essentials of a voluntary and several power.

VI

I conclude with a brief study of the objection that matter, or physics, in some of its forms, has power to *coerce* a free, or voluntary, activity. That our bodily organs deliver up to mind external impressions, I have cheerfully conceded, from the beginning. I now affirm that these impressions, be they ever so vehement when acting normally, are but a preliminary and, so, only an exciting cause ministering to mind, never an efficient cause born with discursion and volition; that matter and physics can do many things for me, in order to what I can do myself, and that having done all they can for me, I am left free to fall back upon my own resources, and act with cognitive efficiency.

There is, and can be, no clashing of principles of action between the two.

Besides having a nature of its own, the child is fenced in with external forces and constitutive resources, from birth. It is, as before explained, an organism of mind and external organs acting together, and interacting with a world of outside entities when brought into communication, in pursuance of a fundamental ordinance which confines both within impassable barriers.

The acceptance of these facts silences all cavil. Indeed, the best certified, fundamental fact of the universe is, that mind (our sole witness for any fact) is so declarative of its severalty and discursive freedom, that matter is an affirmed and accredited exterior potency solely on the former's reportorial authority.

But now, if it report matter and physics as an outer something with an equipment of powers not at all cognitive, it must, for a stronger reason, report itself as another something with cognitive and reporting competencies.

Hence, the conclusion is irresistible that a sensation as a physical cause having its departure outside of mind, is never in any condition to act as a discursive cause issuing from the mind alone. But even though it be an outsider, it can act on the former, and at times very violently, as an exterior cause, but never as a conscious energy formulated by the thinker. It may co-act with mind, but it cannot displace the co-acting agent.

In all I have heretofore said, it is to be understood that I have been regarding thought and its exteriorities as co-acting factors engaged in a common work. I am not debating problems growing out of certain pathological conditions which overpower the volitional efficiencies of thought. For, if you put a club into the hands of sensation, the valor of the bravest thought will have to succumb to the assault. Sensation must be full-witted and normal, lest thought be driven from the field.

PART II

THE ACQUISITION OF KNOWLEDGE

CHAPTER VII

THE CRADLE OF THOUGHT

IN former chapters I have aimed to give thought
a conscious freedom in the presence of sensations,
environment, etc. I am now to regard it as a provident, watchful, and active energy, gathering power
as it gathers ideas. Of course, what it does cannot
be a work of its own, unless freely gone upon. And
if freely gone upon, its achievements must found
on antecedents running back to childhood. And,
therefore, should we make a study of the child as
it is being trained in the universe of thought, if
we are ever to have anything approaching a true
account of free determinations.

The child acts as it thinks.

" When I was a child, I spake as a child, I thought
as a child, but when I became a man, I put away
childish things."

Childish things are indeed put away, but in all
essentials of mind and mind-power, the child and
man are one; the same person who thinks and acts
as a child, thinks and acts as a man. The continuity of free discursion is unbroken from infancy to
old age. The mature man is but a renewal of and
advance upon, his immature self. And, therefore,
if it be but this founding of effort on previous ef-

61

forts; this growth upon previous growth; a conscious advance upon, and because of, previous ones,
we are driven to regard the conscious antecedents
of the child as of prime importance, demanding
careful scrutiny. And this I propose to give in
what follows.

I

It were desirable to have our former self present
before us. The pen may fail of doing justice to
such a personage. And, therefore, would I invoke
collaborators to institute a searching re-discussion
of this much neglected branch of psychology. I
begin with a common formula which will express
my views, when taken in reference to the growth
and birth of thought: "The child is father to the
man."

How true! The mature man has no other father.
But the paternity is unlike ordinary generation;
the ancestor is ever along, and one with, the issue.

Inasmuch, then, as the child is thus our father,
and ever one with us, are we not, therefore, hedged
in with a very proximate and tight-fitting heredity?
And should we not feel like renewing his acquaintance and recalling his acts; remembering that, in
recalling them, we are depicting the lineaments of
our former selves?

The child was our earliest teacher, an active
explorer of rarest originality, but what he taught
was what we ourselves discovered. He sought out
things within and without, and, as his wit sharpened, he ventured boldly on a boundless field of

exploration. He would make inquisition of every-thing; peering anxiously into the unknown. In the very beginning he manifested strong rational proclivities, and soon thereafter thought began its active mission. In a moment he awoke to conscious life and its struggles. Thenceforward he was committed to a career of thought and personal effort wherein he wrought out knowledge and gained power from every quarter. And when he came to think, he clearly perceived that he was a power unto himself, in virtue of his own discoveries. Modest, artless, confiding, but open-eyed and expectant, at the start, he becomes, in time, a pronounced, self-reliant energy, dotting the centuries with a galaxy of deeds.

We cannot interrogate too faithfully these initial acts of our child-father. For if he is the parent of our present intelligence, we are now standing on what we did as a child. And we are now partakers of these first things of his mind through the rational discoveries that made them ours in the past.

II

Here I give place to a few remarks on what is now made rudimentary to our hands in the teachings of psychologists.

What are the child's distinctive qualifications?

(1) As to its nature. It is furnished with mental capacities and physical organs, the latter presenting impressions in the brain, many, if not most, of which come from the outer world. The eye,

ear, etc., are physical functionaries having widely disparate peculiarities and objectives. Each is concerned with a work rigorously its own, but together presenting all our diverse sensations within reach of mind.

(2) Now, a word or two in respect of the interaction of the two. Our native mental faculties exist, at first, as mere germs. But soon, some facts are won which arrest attention, and so promote the growth of thought. In this way begins that life-long intercourse between mind and those physical perturbations called sensations, an intercourse which trains the former to such a knowledge of rational marks or evidences as will produce conviction, and power of choice, and action.

(3) Remark the mode and manner of intercourse between these two friendly parties.

Matter has to be in a position to be interviewed. Mind prepares to make its acquaintance. They begin to exchange civilities. When the former impacts mind, the latter takes conscious interest in its visitor, and what manner of creature it may be. One is a conscious force, the other, unconscious. The task of the latter is to present phenomena for the former's scrutiny, and, thereupon, the former begins the work of prying into their contents.

For mind is a conscious, curious, impulsive energy, ready for a venture of some kind, and much given to active exploration. It is neither a phase, nor a mode, nor an activity of matter. It is simply a discoverer of facts, or informations, which it would employ in constructing for itself a life of educated wants and satisfactions. It has no extra-cognitive way of doing anything. It is not inspired. Its office is to examine God's works, and trace their rational coördinations; communing with His mind, and thus affirming ideas, judgments, convictions, etc., on evidence for them. I am restricting mind to its capabilities. It knows nothing outside of acts of seeing, judging, affirming, and doing. It is never helped by an intuition, or any such lawless divinity, outside of a rational apperception of phenomena on sufficient evidence (if indeed any intuition can be in anywise distinct from *perception*). Truth is never so ready made that it can be grasped as furnished knowledge. What is apprehended, or conceived, or *known*, comes of the mind's power to *discover* and *judge* for *itself*.

And in this connection I invite attention to a fundamental law of thought. We can never do justice to freedom, or morality, unless we concede that we have both through our power to evoke all knowledge by rational processes from the beginning, discovering and acting on, and with, what we discover.

Yes, it does look unpromising to initiate thought, on occasion of first locking it out of all information. Still, it has no other way open for a discovery of its unique powers. It begins, face to face, with a boundless realm of things unknown, and, for an instant, may stare blindly at the bewildering enigma. But, as will appear hereafter, this inexorable fact solves the whole problem of free determinations.

F

III

The methods employed by the child in seeking knowledge seem to demand a somewhat careful exposition.

It is conscious and logical from its first start in the field of discovery. We have seen that it plants itself on the power to judge, on evidence. Its life is not one of sheer physical, and vital, awareness. There lies, back of this, quite another endowment, which comes into action as soon as sensations appear in the sensorium, and is brought fully to birth in the first acts of judgment.

The child has rational powers, and acts rationally. It is not shut up to an incipient rationality wherein it is simply receptive of sensations. It is an egoistical personage, walking in the light of what it can see and do for itself. It ponders the informations gathered from all corners of the universe, and then adopts a line of conduct begotten of some reason or choice which fixes the responsibility upon itself; for choice carries the responsible soul along with the thought which decides his acts.

Thus far, our child-father is seen to make fair progress. But further. If knowledge is power, he has that power, and must impress himself on things about him.

And so far as he does this, he is a creative energy, made so by projecting the force of his thought into what he does.

But I may not anticipate discussions reserved for particular treatment.

IV

It is not my purpose to give a detailed account of what the child does at this early period. But its mind is not slow to act; and I may mention, therefore, some few of its first acts. Here, then, is something that touches its soul with a sensation, or a feeling. This physical excitation, named sensation, has been presented in the sensorium, and thought begins its investigation. The result, so far, is that we have both sensation and its instant apprehension, and, let me add, some wildering emotion not as yet securely defined.

We are to bear in mind that the child is just setting out on its first voyage of discovery, and therefore, such purely perceptive finds as it then makes, are a surprise to its infantile intelligence, and so cannot call forth its more thoughtful resources. A brute has sensation, perception, and the concomitant emotions, and sits easy in its duller ways. On the contrary, the child has a soul a little too human to be content with a mere perception, and that densest personal response which we call an undefined emotion. His human judgment begins to act, as it affirms and gathers ideas, and by a slow, but steady growth, secures an unfailing flow of rational and moral convictions and emotions. Of course, on attaining to manhood, his mental powers are more widely constructive and serviceable.

Here I venture another remark relevant to the emergence of these initial phenomena when first presented to the child. If any one can get back of sensations, perceptions, and the emotions thereto belonging, and show me that we come to this knowledge without resorting to some act of *judgment*, be it ever so infantile, then, I shall have to confess to a brief interval in the earliest efforts of mind, in which its powers go forth in the tumult of disorder. But this would adjourn the birth of thought only a moment. Indeed, I am inclined to the belief that, at the moment of birth, and in the freshness and ferment among the mob of sensations, perceptions, and emotions, simultaneously on hand, the child might not have time to frame a judgment squarely rational; but, for that matter, it could not then have had time accurately to square such factors according to any rule. We therefore give the child a childish mental start, and argue from that, and not from a previous, nebulous period, if there be any.

As a matter of course, among the very first rational apprehensions, are those by which the child perceives its own acts. And though these may not be very conspicuously marked by the feature of alternative choice, yet, so far as they involve the slightest attention and judgment, the act is both rational and voluntary. No one will question this. But indeed, if I am not mistaken in affirming the simultaneous irruption of sensation, perception, and some little emotion, there must be some faint glimmerings of choice involved in comparing phenomena so disparate that the feature of diversity could not be eliminated without an act of judgment discriminating and comparing the diverse traits affirmed. And hence the conclusion that neither sensations, nor perceptions, nor emotions, can ever become the child's own rational achievements, until they are made rational constituents of his soul by the power to know and judge them.

In this connection I pause to consider those undefined emotions which arise on occasion of our first knowledge of sensations, and move the child to act before it can take firm hold upon its rational resources.

With idiots, the power of reason is either smothered, or else a total blank. And when this is the case, the sole antecedents to action are, as a rule, sensations, and the equally agnostic emotions. Such antecedents are, therefore, necessitating causes. The same considerations may apply to the child when all its rational powers are in a state of nascent incubation. But when the clarifying power of thought sets in, one would think that the child could remark the blind strivings of its vagrant emotions. And this it does, to a degree, at the earliest moment after it has, once for all, begun to reason. For, whenever it can take up distinct informations, it will act rationally, and be emotioned accordingly, never more relapsing into a plane of action where, seeing and feeling darkly, it must act as it is seeing and feeling. Remark, now, the drift of my exposition. I have granted that, at birth, sensations, emotions, etc., are so utterly new that the child may not know their import, and so not see what to do. And if it could not see clearly what to do, it could not have any well-defined, rational emotion, however much it might be impressed by the sudden entrance of perturbations, then almost wholly vital and animal.

Now, the truth is that such raw sensations and emotions are in a marginal zone of indefinite and indeterminate cognition, and are there, because needed to stimulate effort during the formative period.

Perception of such phenomena, at that time, is necessarily only an inchoate cognition. But, as before explained, thought begins to make their acquaintance, and thinking gives definite informations, and accordant, definite emotions, — voluntary propulsion and responsible conduct, — a type of transformations quite foreign to merely physical and vital causes and effects. For, just as soon as the soul becomes rational, it becomes personal, and soon thereafter moral, having knowledge and the corresponding emotions as guiding and impelling factors in act or deed.

V

It remains now to explain, more particularly, what the child is doing, when busied with the task of affirming and discriminating the things about it. The materials for this discussion are ready to hand.

The mother is one of the first objects to arrest its attention. It touches her, and sees where it touches. It clings to her, muscularly, whilst taking in her superficies and the indications of life and love detected in her movements, voice, etc. It would know the significance of all these sensational phenomena. But at one and the same time, it is regarding, contrasting, coördinating, and appreciating muscular, auditory, tactile, visual, gustatory, and lactile sensations, besides those of deglutition, etc. For, as it is nourished on her breast, it is beholding her person and countenance, hearing her voice and receiving her caresses, etc., etc., with the eager interest of a neophyte.

And these, and similar, experiences are repeated, again and again, with variations innumerable. It has never one sensation by itself. The tribunal of cognition and judgment never adjourns. The onward flow of informations never subsides, and each item is a discovery that lends power to discover more. The nurse; father, mother, brothers, and sisters; the cat, the dog, the chair; the light from the window, the slam of the door, the fall of footsteps, the rose, the cherry, the peach, — each and all enchain its attention. Its feet are cold; the nurse warm; the chair is hard; the peach soft. It smells a bright rose, and tastes a red cherry. It sees the quiet blue, or else the stimulating tints of the bird whose song thrills its soul with unutterable raptures. If the bird perch on its hand it is wooed with regardful eyes and gentle attentions. Its body, build, weight, shape, etc., are distinctly affirmed. It is seen to be alive, and tremulous with vital and muscular movements. The intermittent pulsations proceeding from a thing of life are set off against the less sympathetic visitations of dead matter. The bird sings, and it discriminates the song from mechanical sound.

And the child ponders all these things with deep-ening interest, for they bedew its soul with the light of reason. It remarks any dissimilarities, and ad-judges different traits to be traits of different things, as distinctly different as sensations from thought, or its power. It separates one thing from another, and, as I have said, frames a judgment founded on their discrepant characters. And, herein, it has excogi-tated the idea of an individual thing, by its pecul-iar marks, distinguishing things different by marks which they do not hold in common.

From hence, we may see how our child-father came to have the idea of things different; of self and not self; of matter, mind, and their characteris-tic and contrasting attributes, etc., and how he cor-related ideas with things different by remarking and identifying the diverse features found in each. And having acquired all these and manifold other informations, he must have also acquired the idea of a self-conscious, intelligent, personal power and agency which is his, and not of the things about him.

And so we all have been going to school in that world-wide university built of God, where all His children prepare for the plunge into business, and a life of choice and fearful responsibility. And we all took the same thought-forming and judgment-training courses in original research.

Ah, those inspiring school-days of twenty or twenty-five years we once had in our Father's house, preparing for the battle of life and thought! We set out to discover a universe of things about us, and we brought back a correct report of all we had mind to discover! And we were helped with many a corrective hint, being born again unto the *power* of knowledge!

And the child *is* father to the man.

CHAPTER VIII

Perceptive Presentations

I

Perceptions are the first discursive acts of the child.

It has been explained that, soon after it is born it has quite a large assemblage of objects in hand to arrest its attention, some within itself and some without. Moved by a God-given curiosity, it begins their study, immediately. But it imports thence only an account of what it discovers. As rational, it goes out to investigate phenomena, and, coming into contact with some sensorial perturbations, it affirms and certifies these perturbations, and so returns with nothing but an affirmation of what it has seen, achieving thus an idea or cognition of, say, taste, sound, touch, smell, etc., and it names this perturbation, so perceived, a sensation.

This and its like, is the sum total of what it achieves in an act of perception, external or internal. It perceives, or fetches, the notion of a something it has interviewed. Or, in other words, we may say: Some kind of an energy, which is not that of our thought, is at work in one of our sensor organs, producing an impression there. We remark this impression, and name it a sensation. But the act of affirming a sensation we call perception. Or, to change our perspective slightly, we may say : A change is going on in one of our sensor organs, and we certify this change, by passing a judgment on some of its more obvious traits (for what has none is imperceptible). And so we say, off hand : Well, here is a something whose acts we are witnessing and affirming. And we dub the phenomena, thus witnessed and affirmed, a sensation; and this report of what we saw is perception, or our readiest cognition, affirming and avouching what we have discovered through one or more of our senses.

Similar remarks, *mutatis mutandis*, apply to acts of the observing intelligence. Here, we are cognizing our own thoughts, *perceiving* or affirming ideas, discursions, or operations, of the mind itself.

You observe that all the mind has gained is an idea, or affirmation of the thing interviewed. Perception, then, is a certification and presentation of the ideas uncovered in the simplest inspection of objects.

At a later stage, and on deeper study, mind may succeed in extending its report; perceiving, and presenting additional ideas sought out of a universe of things to be known by their identifying traits.

You see, I am only giving thought its first outing in quest of informations, and speaking, solely, of the first ideas gained by the readiest cognition of things, that is to say, by perception. It is understood, too, that I am not attempting to separate perfectly what is due to perception, and what to conception; a feat more obstructive than profitable.

II

I now bespeak an attentive consideration of what thought does when achieving its first cognitions.

I repeat, for perception, that it simply affirms an object, or else some attribute of the object, be it a sensation, emotion, or any mental operation. For, when we are perceiving, we are framing our first mental outline or report of the object.

And this is our briefest tale, or announcement, of what we have discovered, and it is but a fragment of the abundant informations reached by the more thorough explorations of the logical understanding.

I have also explained that every act of perception founds on an act of judgment which identifies the object by its complement of distinctive marks. It is, therefore, a rational discovery, and because rational, it is reported as such, and kept in store for further scrutiny, and in order to a comparison with other ideas with which it is seen to affiliate.

Among the first ideas acquired are perceptions of self, as actively thoughtful, affected and emotioned; ideas of both body and spirit, and the source whence they come; some, pointing to an exterior object, others, to the conscious energy, and its activities.

We have seen that the child's own soul, and all its surroundings, engage its attention with the prompt impressiveness of things, new and wonderful. And so, being consciously curious, if not touchingly verdant, from the outset, it cannot escape attempting some idea of itself, as active and affected. And I feel that I can venture to say that it has also a special train of ideas connected with itself, such as those of bewilderment, uncertainty, fear, and fearful suspense, and many such like; all which is this same idea of self in a state of emotion which springs from the almost agnostic beginnings of its cognitive explorations.

I am not now descanting upon the difficulty it must have had in achieving the distinct affirmation of sensations. It remains to point out that if it had the emotions referred to above (and if alive at all, it must have had them), then, it must also have had the ideas (be they ever so nebulously formulated) on which to found them, but both ideas and emotions caught up in an instant of startling initiation well-nigh confounding.

Only a moment ago, I mentioned the fact that the mind itself is variously affected by the divergent ideas caught up from the spectacle of outward and inward phenomena, and that these variant ideas beget corresponding emotions.

Now, in contemplating the phenomena of various emotions the mind will not confound one with another, but will distinguish each by its several characters, and thus discretely separate what idea it may have of each emotion from others of the brotherhood, eliminating, finally, a faint first thought of their implication in our personal economy, and so on, distinguishing ideas and emotions from themselves, and from each other, as different objects isolated by marks of contrariety.

Mind alone perceives, and, therefore, delivers, or presents, ideas of sensations, etc., and, because it is emotioned at those ideas, it grasps a new type of ideas; namely, those of the emotions which answer to the call of the ideas previously presented. Now, as otherwise stated, all this is perception, on the apprehension of the mental contraposition of idea as an affirmed cognition, and idea as an affirmed impulse, or emotion, transpiring in the soul.

And in this, mind is a discoverer, identifying, and affirming its finds by the swiftest inspection of their contents.

Moreover, it is to be observed that perception, here as everywhere, concerns a concrete object whose elements await separation by the elaborating processes of analysis and methodical abstraction. Yet, because they come together as idea and emotion, thought and its personal force, you cannot perceive the one without perceiving the other.

Thought affirms the things of itself, and external nature, and reports what it saw and felt. And this is about all it does in an act of perception. And so we may conclude that every idea of self, or not self, is born of some judgment founded on evidence. And if so, then this briskest resource of mind must play an important part, to say the least, in avouching the ideas to be availed of by its more deliberate processes.

CHAPTER IX

Supplementary Statements

I

Looking now toward a final view of the office of sensations in respect of perception, and regarding them at the time when they swim into the mind's horizon, we may ask: What are they, then, to the mind? I repeat, they are wholly a surprise and confusion; the mind at that earliest period of juvenescence affirming only this.

An illustration may serve to make this plain: We are in the presence of some seemingly unbalanced providence, disclosing, say, whimsical, erratic, and stunning accompaniments. What are we to do with it? We cannot divine the rationale of the thing. We are dazed. Such an astonishment is quite beyond our thinking. And the hideous portent remains relentless, until we get a firm hold on its *meaning or mission ;* get some firm grip on the *ideas* of the portent-maker.

Now, it is just so with the first coming sensations of a child. They are *portents,* until relieved by a discovery of some idea which will dispel the mystery.

And never until we can frame some first conjecture, and so have some theory of their meaning, and, it may be, remove some of their darker connotations, can they be aught to us but the direst confusion resulting from our ignorance. Thought dispels the mystery.

Again, sensation is a manifestation of physical power coöperating with that of mind. It may be a monster of dynamics in its way. It can deliver a physical irritation in the sensorium with faultless precision, but never an idea. It cannot overstep the despotism of its limitations, any more than mind can usurp its functions and discharge its offices. While, for its part, the latter can see a sensation, remark its character, and report accordingly, the former, in turn, has no power to report anything in terms of the co-active, discursive factor. Its office is to present a perturbation in one of our sense centres. It has to remain an impalpable factor, unknowing and unknown, an unbalanced visitation, a portent, until mind evolves the story-telling *ideas* that solve the riddle.

II

The preceding discussions have led me to remark upon the simultaneous emergence of sensation and its perception: brain presenting physical impressions, and mind perceiving them; perception and sensorial perturbations taking place co-actively and coëtaneously.

But we may further consider this problem of perception, and its exteriorities, from another point of view: All these sensor impressions are involuntary.

Consider the sense of hearing, for a moment. The ear is so constructed that it conveys an external vibration to the inner sensorium, causing there a physical irritation, or perturbation. Here, the immediate object perceived is this irritation, an object presented by the auditory organ, not by the mind. This physical object, so presented, is therefore involuntary.

Similar remarks apply to other physical organs. They all present, or deliver their several impressions, often violently, but, when acting normally, with a degree of conservative vigor just sufficient to give thought a fit object for the display of its rational, volitional, and personal powers.

You may have observed that I am distinctly admitting that an exterior impression is delivered to me with a vigor adequate to attract my attention, affording me an opportunity thus to react on it, as best I may, with the powers of my voluntary and constructive knowledges. And, confessedly, this does give me a physical object for my study, and which my thought could never give. Moreover, if an exterior potency is ever to be at all known, it must in some way be presented as an object for thought, lest otherwise, if I had to present it, I must needs be exterior to myself to make the exterior presentation.

I am not, however, to be driven to the conclusion (conventional usage to the contrary) that the sensor organ is sensitive. Its sole office is to deliver sensations.

The cognitive activity alone is sensitive. The

outward organ mediates a physical impression after
its own way, and thereupon the former, ever open
to the call of external visitations, consciously and
sensitively apprehends it.   The exterior visitation
neither imports sensitiveness, nor a susceptibility
to sensation, but the mind gets it *from within*, ere it
can be properly equipped for going out to affirm the
sensorial visitation.

But this apart, we have now some sensorial objects before the bar of thought, and having these,
we are prepared to enter upon all our rational possibilities, affirming ideas or knowledges by affirming
the attributes which identify the objects presented.
For, if we have objects for thought, we may discursively re-integrate their rational constituents
and affiliations.

III

Here I am led to inquire: How can we know sensations?   Allow me to offer a brief explanation.
As phenomena, they would forever remain an unknown quantity, if we could not see some tracings
of *meaning;* some touches of thought and method;
something significant in their behavior stamped in
their constitution.   And it is a matter for mind to
note these tracings and make report of their value.
If it can decipher the underlying meanings, and so
get out the significance of the tracings, it will have
something for its pains, an idea, opinion, or information which it can affirm and act on.

For the acquisition of any knowledge is just so
much power achieved for shaping an order of con-

secutions well known to constructive thought. And the principle on, or by, which anything was constructed, is open to exploration, and will reveal in what it is, and does, some intimations of the mind that constructed it; and so, if we would interpret his work, we must proceed from it to the thought of him who planned it, just as we do when we proceed from human works to human thoughts, for an explanation more or less satisfactory.

But can this explain how we know sensations? Yes! The fetch of ideas from any of our sensorial impressions, as from the more stupendous works of creative thought; what is it at bottom, but to discover God's constructive and creative ideas hid away in sensations, phenomena, portents, or anything else that can lay claim to distinctive attributes?

And if, peradventure, we should ever come to know them they would have to be laboriously sought out and dug up, after the manner of one excavating antique finds.

And what if, in this regard, mind should be the expert archæologist who studies the finds, deciphers the inscriptions, and certifies and publishes their import! For what we all find is "hid treasure" awaiting discovery and interpretation, and many a link in the concatenation may never be found.

But then, our epigraphist is curious, enthusiastic, enterprising, and much emotioned in view of results, and never halts until he has laid bare the last secret meet for his day and generation.

For these, and similar reasons, therefore, we feel

justified in concluding that our thought, as seen in the perception of sensations, or other objects, is but the perception of some thought, or the evidence for it, stowed away in phenomena, sensorial, or other. It is human thought discovering the thought of some other thinker.

An abundant practical experience engenders a safe, common-sense capacity for recognizing and making use of evidences of mind and meaning seen in things exterior.

And we soon find that the more successfully we do this, the truer we are to the mother nature of our own constructive thought and to that of universal creation as well.

CHAPTER X

CONCEPTIVE PRESENTATIONS

I

THE discovery of bare (concrete) ideas, or their presentation, may be fraught with vivid satisfactions, and still the soul may not be the efficient, provident, personal energy it becomes when it can take full charge of conduct. At this latter period, it is moved by the power of more comprehensive, and, therefore, more productive, informations. It is hence incumbent on us to remark upon some particulars of its progressive work, if we would know how it wins its way to freedom.

We have just seen it acquiring a large store of perceptive informations. It is, therefore, now in a position to bethink itself of further conquests. And our purpose is to keep along with it as it extends its inquiries. And, though we have been consciously affirming its feats, from infancy onward, its way to advanced achievement well-nigh forbids any satisfactory statement.

II

Mind alone is sensitive, the sensor organ, not. The latter, however, delivers itself dynamically, and lodges an impression within reach of the power which, in turn, first feels, and then perceives, the impression.

Now, at the very moment of perception, some dim pencillings of discursive thought must begin to emerge, heralding the advent of wider vistas beyond mere perception, but, as yet, too shadowy for the bold outlines of conception. Let us call this vague blushful premonition of conception, the notion, because, though a real knowledge, it has not been distinctly clarified and affirmed by the searching scrutiny of analysis and judgment. For we must take it that our larger, rational competencies have been bestowing, at least, a curious interest in those earliest discoveries of perception, and so have turned up some discursive intimations, darkly, yet joyfully, at their worth, and are now at the door of conception, peering beyond.

I would not be misunderstood. Every achievement of mind is, in fact, more or less discursive. Even perception, being, as before explained, a presentation by the *judgment,* is, for that reason, a first, or primary, inference, or discursion. This remark covers every information mediated by the test methods of judgment and inference, on inspection of evidence.

It will therefore be my aim to follow up the psychological development of knowledges so deliberately entered upon in preceding pages, dwelling on that particular stage reached by the mind when it is seeking those of wider significance than mere perceptions, but restricting our inquiry more to a view of them as discoveries, than as *potencies.* (The latter will be dealt with later on.)

For indeed, the soul is so indivisibly a unit that, when it is discursive, it is potent, and when potent, discursive. It is always alive to the *power* of its thoughts; both conception and its power supervening on occasion of a view of its growing wants and interests, a class of personal requirements so eminently human, that they never manifest themselves save as they respond to the call of the strictly human thoughts that inspire them.

III

But to proceed with my analysis of the bolder flights of conception! The problem before us is to determine how thought ever comes to know enough of itself, and the things about it, to enable it to conceive, and realize, its higher wants. I instance some familiar examples. Here is an old illustration, that of a rose. An exact analysis forbids our saying, we *perceive* it. When first confronted, we perceive only the excitations made in the sensorium, namely, those of sight, taste, smell, etc., and as we said, these begin to take discursive transformation, tremulously and vaguely, in the notion.

But thought hies onward. In the act of perception, it feels the awakening stimulus of concrete ideas, and, in the same instant, takes the road to conception in the light of the faint glimmerings of the notion. And now, if we would know more of it, we must needs keep abreast with its bolder visions beyond.

The rose emits an effluvium which travels along the olfactory nerves to the inner sensorium, there

to meet the power that perceives it as an object to
be known, and object for study.   Here the resources
of comparison, judgment, and inference are brought
into requisition, and begin an eager, and tireless,
inquiry.

See the result!   The sensation is touched with
some differentiating features (it could not be anything without these).   They are identified as constituent elements, or, else, qualifying adjuncts,
of the rose, and if so, they are the attributes, or
accompaniments, which mark it as an individual
thing distinct from other things.   Here we have
uncovered many informations, correlated, distin-
guished, contrasted, called forth at the bidding of
thought.

Here, too, in the grouping of such contrasting
and divergent phenomena, we have some of our
first conceptions: of the related and dependent;
of a whole and its parts; of an exterior force and
what it does, and of that peculiar relation of mind
as a discoverer of facts to the object which it inter-
views.

Such are some of the conceptions of thought;
brave achievements with suggestive, constructive,
far-reaching affiliations.   Whence come they?   Why
here, why studied, and what their import?   Can
we connect them with human wants ?   Can they
be employed in life and conduct, as our exertive,
and personal, motors ?   The answer to these questions may be gathered from what follows.

For the present, we are but spectators, beholding
thought acquiring the knowledge on which it may

found character and conduct; its efficiency, as a free cause, being measured by the scope and bear-ing of its informations. For in affirming certain attributes as part and parcel of the things of, or about, us, we are employing our own distinctively rational method for ascertaining what they are and what they do; affirming thus a brotherhood of members and traits which may be resolved into their identifying marks, and put to such a discur-sive use as will minister to our higher wants. For thought is ever making discoveries in the interest of its loftier appreciations.

The rose impacted the sensorium with a physical impression, and thought discovered its significance It fetched forth ideas of cause and effect, self and not self, external power with its train of variously significant impressions. It was given a concrete perturbation in a sensor organ or organs. It decom-posed this into the parts of the concrete thing that contained them. It has contrasted an exterior po-tency with its own inner potencies. It has conferred with the rose, and ascertained that it is fragrant, beautiful to the eye, ministering to our æsthetic satisfactions. And so, again, it has compared notes with its colors, and configuration, and garnered up ideas of touch and sight combined. And it will bring in the soft, the hard, the smooth, the rough, etc., and connecting all these knowledges together by a con-ception of their æsthetic, utilitarian, or other pecul-iarities, pass onward to considerations which will arouse our higher emotional and voluntary suscep-tibilities.

It would be more than tedious to make mention of every idea, sought out from a study of the rose, and its relation to ourselves, and other entities. But there are some associated with the universe of things around us, which claim a passing notice in this connection. It is but one of numberless things, all of which are naturally so interdependent that, whilst proclaiming this mutual dependence, they proclaim, as well, the creative thought of Him who conceived and constructed their being, and apportioned, and correlated their diverse functions.

And here, it is needless to say that in all this effort to command the meaning of the things we are interviewing, we are evoking conceptions of laws of being and action resting on the thought of the first Lawgiver.

IV

But again, we have seen perceptions diverge and differ, parting off into distinct classes, answering to the external organs which mediate diverse impressions. And we may have noticed that even those which belong to the same class have many striking points of dissimilarity. Now, all these divaricating traits enounce the salient marks which attract attention.

What, then, is the attitude of a young mind in such a presence? It is in a land of wonders, expectant and deeply emotioned. It will, therefore, feel that it has a marvel of strange things to unravel. It will not long remain in suspense. It will

at once begin their investigation, by sorting out the
component elements of the different impressions, —
some of which are statical, and some dynamical, —
arriving finally at some settled convictions on which
it may act.

Yet, this is but one of the numberless similar
problems to which it gives due attention all through
life, and in order to a further conception of what
they are, and what to do with them.

Another point may here be dwelt upon.

Not infrequently, exterior forces present themselves intrusively, — sometimes violently. Now,
it will behoove thought to see, not simply what
they are in barest presentation, but, as I have said,
to come to some conclusions in respect of their behavior and meaning, and give them place as so much
mental power that may be put to use for our personal betterment.

It is readily seen that we are here alighting on
some informations bearing on the conservation of
life, health, morals, business, etc. And it is for
this reason that the very lineaments of our various
sensations have to be understood and placed in their
logical connections. The coördination of sensations
with their causes, the sedulous study of every potency, — our own and other's, — with a view to the
growth of our own conscious powers, all these have
to be caught up, and matured, and fixed in the soul.

V

The sheet of paper on which I am writing may
serve to exemplify the general subject of concep-

tion. If one sees but the awkward, shambling chirography, he gets but scant information. But let us give it, and its tortuous tracings in ink, a little careful thought. Is that all we see? All indeed, if we have only perceptive informations. But our thought is a restless energy, given to more rational ventures. It has a wide range of inquisitive powers by which it acquires discursive informations. It is by no means a weak-minded neophyte taking the veriest outside view of the fixtures and features of things about him.

It discovers that these letters form syllables, words, sentences, paragraphs, etc.; that their allocation on the paper gives them a grammatical structure, and that, together, they are signs of the thought of the writer, which any reader may recast.

Remember, that all we started with was paper, ink, and cursive characters. But what have we now beyond these? Many things: thought, penmanship, rhetoric, grammar, logic, opinion, judgment, and many other debilitating effusions. But we follow the conceptive affiliations of the argument so faithfully that we have rethought the thoughts of the thinker.

We have sifted the scrawl and released its rational constituents. The writer gives us a sample of his work, and we put our mind to work upon it, and affirm and follow his thoughts. And this, his work, was withal a new creation, not made over to him by a neighbor, but a work of his own, formulated and finished by force of the inborn power of his conceptions.

And you, his readers, what in turn are you doing? Your eyes see only the paper, ink, and cursives. But you give them discursive appreciation. You separate them off by their literary, logical, and other rational consanguinities. And in this you are remarking the writer's thought, on evidence for it. You found it wrapped up in the unconscious cerements of ink and paper, and now, behold, it is alive and speaks!

And in this regard, you too have been doing what I call a creative work, brought home to your hand by the power of discursion. For though you may not create anything, *de novo*, yet your power of thought has brought to you a *new* thing, that in all cases exists for you, only through your power to conceive it.

VI

I come now to a study of, say, an apple. We touch, taste, see, smell, and feel it, mediating thus diverse impressions, and framing variant ideas of its peculiar attributes. Here is progress, but so far, only bare perceptions, or else, inarticulate conceptions, in aid of these. But now, if we undertake to compare and contrast these impressions, we are invoking the giftlier resources of mind. We are bringing up the reserves and body-guards of the soul.

We remark that the apple is connected with the parent stem; the bud with the bloom; bud and bloom with the fruit; the fruit with its power to please the taste, or to sate hunger; the bud, bloom, branches, etc., with the main trunk, etc. The sap, the seasons, the fertile soil, the abounding world around us, all are thoughtfully pondered, and the purport of their interrelations sought out and affirmed. For we are in search of the finger prints of constructive thought stamped on nature, and we have only to recognize them, in order to the assumption of constructive powers of our own.

And, therefore, do we make requisition of all our rational resources, and so reach conclusions, convictions, dianoetical informations, etc., and act as these inform us. And I repeat, we reach the aforesaid power of knowledge by a rational elaboration of the things we study, that is to say, by a conception of their statical and dynamical affiliations with our personal good (or bad).

VII

We now work our way to the horse, another capital find. But how did we ever come to discover our way out to him? He is not without some points of attraction within easy call of mind. Our optic nerves receive his visual outlines, and deliver them to the inner sensorium, where they are perceived. But can thought release their meaning? Its mission is to pry into the why and the wherefore of things, in order to personal power. It will therefore try to know the horse, and its capabilities. It sees that its configuration cuts it away from other objects in the landscape. It follows the peculiar profile from which we frame the mental map of an animal, in contradistinction to what is not one, and so on, discriminating, finally, one horse from another, and from other things. Here many conceptions are summoned forth, in understood connections.

But thought halts not. It sets foot forward on new and ever newer ground, advancing from conquest to conquest. It affirms the color of the horse, its grade, and shading; and compares these with other colors of the brood and of the landscape. Then, there is its physique, bristling with the signs of life in all its members. These are likewise distinctly pondered and formulated. But it is put to repeated acts of judgment, in making out the parts which identify the horse, and, at the same time, distinguish it from other horses, or things. And here it is, at the same moment, acquiring many other ideas, such as those of proof and inference from the evidences, verification of facts, and conviction, etc. Here, too, it comes to know the position, posture, *ubi*, and habits of the animal in rest or motion, each and all of which have to be distinctly affirmed before they can be rated as conceptions.

Should we inquire now: Whence all these fruitful discoveries? The answer is: They are the faithful products of discursive reason. The two diverse factors concerned are mind, and the entities that confront it. Each is a power unto itself, but neither can derogate from what is competent to the other. What is of the horse, and its surroundings, conveys impressions to the inner sensorium, just as what is of the mind affirms all it can see and interpret of the outness, locality, life, ways, utilities, marks, etc., of the horse.

The horse has life and power, power of muscle and thought, and what he does, and is, are indicia of his capabilities. He is hence a find which we can train to serve us in many industrial, and even æsthetic ways, and to an almost unlimited extent. He is docile, tractable, strong, durable, serviceable, and when we come to know all these things, we can make use of him as a domestic animal.

VIII

The great problem of how we come to conceive the idea of *cause* comes next in order.

It is plain that we cannot act our part in life's stirring drama without knowing that we have *power* to act it. It is equally plain that we cannot perform it without a knowledge of the power of neighboring entities. Action expresses cause, or productive energy, and implies a subject acting, and an object acted upon.

Now, the peculiarity of thought is that, when acted upon by an exterior cause, it cannot receive the action of its correlate with absolute passivity. For, when once in cognitive commerce with such an object, it goes out to meet it with a cognitive vehemence peculiar to itself, and adapted to the emergency. It acts on what it knows, and according to what it knows, of the power and mission of its visitor.

But the very first act it bestows on its visitor is an act of attention which is an act of the will, and, therefore, a personal *cause.*

But I am presently to inquire : How get we the idea of an *external* cause ?

I have just pointed out the fact, that, when an external object produces an impression on some one of our inner sense centres, thought actively, and instantly, perceives that impression as a power external to the power that affirms it; for an external object has been presented for its study. And when it resolves this impression into a subject and its attributes, abstracting, for closer inspection, the several potencies and adjuncts that constitute it, it could not long stand firm against the partition of such constantly recurring phenomena as antecedence and subsequence into *power and result,* which is the idea of cause and effect.

For, indeed, to speak of a thing as lacking the attribute of power or cause, is to speak of what we are unable to conceive ; and this, because nothing in the universe can come into conception, save through some manifestation of its *power.* Some exterior impressions are indeed very mild, some violent, but even the mildest must present some trace of power, adequate to make the impression in the sensorium, on perceiving which, thought perceives an external potency.

The fact is patent, therefore, that we have our idea of an external cause from a series of external impressions, made in the sensorium, and whether mild or violent.

If they are sufficiently forceful to arrest attention to their frequent occurrence, the mind will observe that fact, and, for a while, it may be, ob-

H

serve nothing more. But it may afterward remark upon the constant, and invariable sequence between a given antecedent and subsequent. This will foster a desire to make a more thorough examination. And, so, the mind pauses to account for a priority and posteriority, perpetually recurring, between phenomena, and makes the discovery that there is something more than mere priority in the antecedent; that it cannot act at all, unless potent, and that if potent, its power will be manifested, and even measured, by what it does, *i.e.*, by its result.

Now, I have just explained that we have already had the idea of a *conscious* cause through attention, and acts of judgment and reason. For every act of thought is an act of personal power, going forward as cause, into its peculiar results. It is personal efficiency, or voluntary power. And allow me to say that, when we get this idea of personal *power*, or cause, we are disporting ourselves within the domain of reason and judgment on evidence, and, if we should employ the same idea and the same rational processes to help us to infer an external cause or power sufficient to determine *both* priority and result, it will be but another exercise of reason and judgment, and entirely at our discretion.

Now, inasmuch as a conscious act of reason affirms that this thing named cause, or power, and which is affirmed in affirming any and everything, is an exterior something, and not of ourselves, and, yet, we are certain of having traced the attribute of efficiency to the antecedent which produced the consequent, it follows that we have conceived a cause, or power, in the antecedent sufficient to produce the result. In other words, we have found *power* in the antecedent which sets forth a new something called a result or consequence, which in turn sets forth, and makes good, its claim to the antecedent as the parent energy that went forth to establish it. But, in all this, we are governed by the test methods of observation, comparison, judgment, and inference. Indeed, we have to make conquest of all this cognoscible universe, precisely as we have done with the rose, the horse, etc. For what is presented to our confronting intelligence; what is furnished by any sensorial contributor, — all this is, as I have said, buried treasure whose significance has first to be winnowed out, and then carefully worked up into inferences, convictions, and reconstructive informations, and then finally fixed in character and vented in conduct, and in the moral rectifications and repressions of conscience.

IX

Another step forward in the line of our researches brings up the principle of universal causation expressed in the formula: Every change which begins to exist, or appear, has a cause. And the question presents itself: How does the mind come to know this truth ? Well, just as it affirms everything else, on evidence deemed valid.

We are advancing simply from particular causes

to a supreme cause dominating all particular causes. But this is a search for the power that spake the worlds into being and placed them under orders to an irrepealable *law* of cause and effect.

We had some reasons for determining the law for individual instances of cause and effect, and we discovered a *power* in the antecedent which accounted for the changes observed, and now, we would contemplate one that dominates all changes, and we say with Shakespeare —

> " I'll see these things !
> They are rare, and wondrous *curious*."

Yes, let us see them. But how shall this be done ?

We look within and without and see a vast assemblage of finite powers, and we remark the fact of our inability to frame a system of laws for changes embracing the universe. And yet we see that the whole world is under bonds to some potency which will account for all its transformations, and though finite, we are held to some convictions, honestly acquired. We know that the finite is incompetent to universal power, and we search for something that is. We are inquisitive, and pursue the inquiry.

We see that the work is superhuman and super-finite, and we conceive an adequate power from what such work teaches us. We are in quest of a law of *order* for a universe of changes, the conception of a vast multitude of things grouped together and co-acting under a law of cause and effect such as we affirm for the particular changes we have observed.

We have long since learned that the idea of externality is founded on the potency of the impression, or sensation, made in the inner sensorium. And we argue that a universal cause calls for an all-embracing energy, competent to dominate a universe of changes. And in the strictest analysis, the principle of universal causality is, therefore, but the force of some omniscient thought expressed in all His works, and this supreme, causative efficiency, thus gone over into all manner of changes, is the antecedent cause which conceived, and constructed, and continually enforces, a universal law of causation for all things finite.

It is to be understood that we do not pretend to follow every thought and every turn of thought that goes into any work, finite or infinite. And yet, it is simply impossible to behold the transformations going on in phenomena, and not affirm one thing: *power of some kind, in any, or all, antecedents, competent to produce the result, or results.*

We are utterly unable to ignore such an insuperable presence. We can conceive of no change but what is under bonds to a power adequate to produce it.

X

But now, that the regular coördination of entities has had incidental mention, I may inquire, further, in respect of how we conceive a rational basis for the interplay of their activities.

If, in the display of their activities, they pursue an accepted order of transformations, there must be some reasons why they evince such an order. As neighboring entities coming within reach of the mind's power to apprehend them, they must have some way of making themselves knowable to the power that undertakes to know them; some way of mutely intimating their presence and attributes to our thinking possibilities.

Inquiring, then, why mind can discourse with matter, we have but one possible answer: Matter has a tell-tale sign-language of her own, implanted in her constitution and manifested in her attributes. She is, indeed, not given to talk, but she can present phenomena so charged with meaning and rational coördination that our thought can lay hold on these and make use of their rational intimations. For this earlier, and non-verbal, speech of matter has its parallel in man's acts, or deeds, and is known as we know them.

But, being what it is through the thought of an omniscient thinker, our finite thought can remark the evidences of his shaping intelligence behind and beyond the phenomenal manifestations.

The truth is that all knowledge, and all science, founds on a concerted arrangement for the commerce of mind, as a discoverer of truth, and matter, as the work of some other mind. And, therefore, is it that no phenomena can ever be certified and explained except on condition of our finding some other mind, speaking to us through the rational economy of order displayed in the things interviewed.

Talk as we may, there is some pre-adaption in

the things about us by which they speak to us and
vindicate a rational explanation. And it is ever in
this way that our thought discovers in matter (or
in mind in all its moods) some thought or power of
thought of some other thinker, and does really commune with Him as with an elder brother; for it
cannot commune with anything, if its speech is
estranged from the rational principles on which
itself founds.

And therefore comes it to pass that, albeit everything not ourselves is an outsider, it can be entreated as a familiar whom we may interrogate and
deliver of his ideas, after the manner of the redoubtable Socrates. For what is orderly, is so, because
of reasons for it, and its speech is rational, because
all work tells some tale of its constructor to any
mind that can afford to frame a thought, or devise
a work of its own.

It is for reasons like these we claim that, when
by an act of conception, we affirm certain attributes
as part and parcel of a given object, we are in fact
affirming that they are held together by the unre-
laxing grip of law and order.

Allow an illustration to the point. We are looking at a photograph. What do we see? Nothing
but the superficies of paper and carpentry work,
every whit matter. At the same moment, however,
our intelligence will be searching for the evidences
of design, meaning, or motive for its construction.

Now, exactly the same method is pursued when
we wish to interpret nature. At first, as before
explained, she is nothing to us but a physical exci-

tation in the sensorium; a something exterior to our perceptive intelligence. But being under charge of a pervading law of order, she speaks for, and vicariously proclaims, an omniscient Lawmaker, as the true cause of everything subject to that law. And now, if we avail ourselves of these explanations, we may approach the problem of universal causation under guide of evidences which compel us to infer the power of creative thought, in order to account for a law of cause and effect impressed upon everything we know of His work.

Yes, there must be power in the antecedent sufficient to produce the result; else otherwise, there could be no change, no result, no universe even.

XI

And right here we are face to face with an objection that impeaches the logic of our contention.

The point is made that, when we infer universal causation from particular instances of it, there is more in the conclusion than in the premises. It will take but a moment, I am persuaded, to expose the fallacy of this famous argument. The logic of particular facts is sufficient for any conclusion we make, and for our part, we would not have it disturbed. We may at least see that there is no more invalidity in the inference to a universal cause pervading all things and all changes, than in inferring many things on which everybody acts, but the truth of which is beyond any possibility of verification by an actual observation of the fact inferred.

For instance, we infer that the sun will rise to-morrow, though we may never step out of the present into the future to get the fact from actual observation before sunrise to-morrow. And you can no more verify this than the fact of universal causation. It is an inference from the fact that the sun has risen every morning up to the present time. But it would be well for the objector to remark that this inference is validated only by conceiving the law for cause and effect to be founded on a power sufficient for *any time*, if not repealed; the implication being that, if God were to withdraw the law for this order of consecutions, our inference would then be that the sun would *not* rise to-morrow.

Here we see that the mind is so conservative in its deductions, that it will not have the inference to be irresistible, except on condition of the law for the return of day and night continuing as in the ages past. The limits of the premises and conclusion are throughout co-terminous. The conclusion is legitimate. A part of what is known to be an order of consecutions implies the whole, as long as that order is unrepealed. Our logic is consistent. Again, from seeing the front of the moon, we infer it has a back, though no man can ever see it. Here our inference is from a direct inspection to what can never be verified by observation. But who doubts, or can doubt, the legitimacy of our inference? The inference is valid. But why? The fact is that, when knowledge is of a part, or parts, we reason to the complementary part, or parts, as well in order to be rational, and even logical, as in order to the whole, and its parts; for we cannot conceive the one without the other. Now, the argument is identical, when, from observing that the sequence of cause and effect obtains among all things knowable, we infer that the law is universal. And yet this is but to infer from a part of God's works to the whole, though we can never see the whole.

Here too, premise and conclusion are consistent. *The part implies the whole.*

But we may vary our argument, so as to state it in the form of a syllogism.

(1.) If there is an order of things *seen* to evince the law of cause and effect, there is a rational cause to account for this order. Now this argument is nowise different from that which finds a back to the moon. It proceeds from a part known by observation — that is to say, particular instances of cause and effect — to a part that can never be known by any amount of human observation. For, if you are compelled to infer cause or power to account for particular results, you are compelled, as well, to infer cause or power sufficient to account for universal results. The logic is irresistible.

(2.) We may state the major premise for universal causation somewhat thus : If the Creator should put matter and mind, *so far as we know them,* under control of a law of cause and effect, the inference is irresistible that they will be similarly controlled so far as this creation extends; supposing all the time that what He has created discloses the consecutions of cause and effect, —

productive power and the result produced, — patterned after the manner of those of any mind, capable of projecting the power of thought into what it can do. For all thought is bound by a law of order — discursive, logical, or other — without which it could not affirm anything.

And here again, we are but bringing in the back of the moon along with the front, — a *logical inference* from some particular fact, or facts, observed, to others incapable of observation. For the argument proceeds upon the fact that a rational power cannot contradict reason, or in other words, the logical sweep of the evidence; and that our inference is valid, when we advance from a part to the whole of an order of transformation co-extensive with all we can affirm of God's works and intelligence, — even though we may never know, by direct observation, any more about this order of things than we know about the centre of the earth, or the centre of the solar system, or the back of the moon; all which is affirmed on evidence from particular facts.

This argument supposes also that we are computing with the effective work done in conformity with a law of causation which evidences the force of some constructive and creative thought, as seen in all we have observed in the special consecutions of cause and effect, — even power in the antecedent specially qualified to produce the unique result.

Tons of coal burning in the open air at the city of Baku will never send a car to Tashkend. But constructive thought will. But wherefore! Because it is taught of the lore of omniscience, caught up from particular instances of cause and effect; because we have remarked and affirmed the consecutions of cause and effect in what we know of ourselves and the external world; because we can argue from any work we see to the measure and quality of a mind, or man, we cannot, or do not see, —and we act as our logic impels us. We *infer* and do, and do as we infer.

XII

I conclude this branch of our subject with some general observations.

Mind can affirm evidences of mind. But this mind must do more than simply observe phenomena. It must pass beyond the phenomenal manifestations of truth, if it would be a constructive power. It must advance from the evidences in hand, to truths beyond the reach of observation, but supported by the evidence. The light and smoke that flicker in a lime-kiln are certainly a conspicuous small fact, readily seen. The unseen core of fire within, without which there had been no smoke and no flicker, is the real efficient of the work done; so, of all work, we must affirm power of some kind in the antecedent specially qualified to produce a given result.

The time for all this loud talk about science, small facts, agnosticism, etc., giving us *all* truth, has passed. I say candidly that these facts are important, as evidences for facts placed beyond the reach of any number of such scientific, but agnostic,

discoveries. The purely phenomenal is not synony-
mous with either entire being or thought. Nature
has a logic of her own planted in her statics and
dynamics — a law for the interaction of all entities
— which inhibits our sundering the evidential from
the facts which they evidence, the part from the
whole, the outer from the inner, the phenomenal
from the real, the portent from the portent-maker.
The phenomenal, the outer, etc., must be chased to
its source in some more pregnant fact.

And so we are brought again to our old conclusion that, when thought is affirming the significance of things lingering in all manner of work
and being it is, in one way or other, recasting the
thought of Him who informed all His works with
countless traces of constructive thought.

Here I would be allowed to make incidental mention of some conceptions resorted to in connection
with our personal well-being.

For we have to discover, not alone, how to make
use of our own faculties and of things not ourselves,
but how to meet wants all of which depend on cal-
culation, judgment, and foresight; wants which can
have no being, until mediated and authorized by
some rational conception of our higher needs. And
it is so that, whenever any advanced conception is
reached, the mind becomes a mightier power, and,
by an exercise of its then mightier powers, wins for
itself an order of constructive informations, more
and more potent, to the end.

And, therefore, thought is not a mere inclosed
subjectivity, content with the literary aspects of its

acquisitions, but a self-conserving energy, discovering informations whose salient function is a constructive support for conduct.

Moreover, thought has some conceptive and constructive intimations, vaguely outlined from the very beginning of its acquaintance with external nature, as I have heretofore explained in other connections. For whatever an external impression may mean, that meaning has to be excogitated of mind, and all the connotations underlying the sensorial impression have to be remarked, and wrought out, solely by a careful sifting of the evidences for them; that is to say, we search for them, and if peradventure we affirm them, they are avouched by more rational conception of the facts which evidence them.

And, therefore, have I explained that they are not seen by an external organ for perception, but by a power of discursive vision which unfolds and affirms attributes in objects, wherein we descry some evidence of the mind of Him who constructed them; this being His way of bringing a product of His thought into communion with ours. For there is, in whatever confronts our intelligence, a constructive make-up of significant attributes that tells some tale of its maker, and so evidences some aspect of His thought.

And it makes no difference, whether we know an object by perception or conception, if only we have a valid conviction resting on evidence; and to the knowing intelligence the only proof of a fact is the evidence of thought seen in the constructive behavior of things, their special attributes and correlations.

Certainly, nothing could be more absurd than to say we could think, much less converse with, an object void of any rational construction. It must have attributes and potencies so correlated as to provoke rational scrutiny.

It seems evident, therefore, that the field of exploration, in which we gather all our ideas, must be built up with significant traits which will avouch some rational story of Him who built it up. It is also evident that, if we did not have this rational basis for discovery and interpretation, we could never acquire those constructive and prospective informations which enable us to block out a line of conduct for a future day. For depending from this power to interpret such characteristic phenomena is the power to witness for aims and purposes which pass over into all we do, and so in turn manifest our own thoughts.

But I now turn to another chapter, where my contention may be further explicated.

CHAPTER XI

MORAL CONCEPTIONS

THE work of a responsible being is totally different from that found in the realm of matter. It is likewise diversely separated from the subordinate processes which develop the intelligence. It is to be hoped that a correct account of that work can now be given.

I

I am presently to contemplate mind in the attitude of conceiving *moral informations*. Having these, we act in view of ends or purposes, and can take pains to secure them. But if we lack these informations, we part company with the last vestige of our nobler humanities.

Man is a personal unit that combats all comers, in order to maintain moral views and aims; that cultivates, and allows for the action of, exterior potencies, whilst commanding their services; that values equally the moral qualities of thought and conduct, devising thus what he shall do, in view of the moral sanctions evoked, and a personal assumption of his obligations.

And here we have achievements quite beyond the range of involuntary transformations, not to mention such pupillary training as the mind resorts to in preparation for moral work. For we are taking man as now prepared to enter the province of morals, where the power to choose enables him literally to carry out his inclinations, or else control them by a different conception of what he ought to do. He has choice in selecting his way of life, and cannot divest himself of it, even if he would. And choice makes him free. Still he must choose under stress of his moral obligations. Observe, he is not under any constraint to emotions, and desires, operating as forces *independent* of the moral conceptions that inspire them. The whole thing is determined by a pressure coming from his moral appreciations; by his ideas of right and wrong. Nor does he ever do wrong through an original impetus which supplants an intelligent foresight of consequences for which he holds himself responsible. The pressure is due to the force of his moral conceptions alone; conceptions whose stringency he has himself mediated and sanctioned.

And here, it may be needful to remark that the general explanation for all the acts of man lies in his power of mind.

I give place to a pertinent illustration of this. Sun and rain operate on a lump of clay, and it is modified, say, to the extreme limit of necessitating causes. These present a number of reactions prescribed by God's unchanging laws, giving us the power and play of involuntary forces. But the behavior of a voluntary or moral potency displays a conscious contrast with that of the former. "The potter hath power over the clay, of the same lump

I

to make a vessel unto honor, and another unto dis-
honor "; commanding thus a result denied to a
material agency.

II

But the point I am now making does not rest
solely on man's power of successful reasoning. It
is an easy inference that animals can do the same
to the extent of their arrested capacities, and to
that extent they are quite as free as man. What
then makes the latter so preëminently human, and
therefore distinct from them? Let us see! He
begins life without any knowledge. In a moment
he is seeking it eagerly. For he has to discover
everything for himself, in order to a hold on his
own way of life, so that what he does is what his
discoveries lead him to do.

Indeed, if his informations had been delivered to
him by a direct infusion of divine illumination, and
without his power of deliberate scrutiny and sanction, he would not have even the faintest hint of
the functions of a free agent. And furthermore, if
he had all knowledge at birth, he could not be free
after the manner of our discursive humanity, unless
perchance he had some way of comparing different
moral traits, and exercising some elective, or else
repressive, vehemence, in choosing between them.

Moreover, if his singular faculty of thought did
not bring within his reach manifold informations
inaccessible to animals, he would be an animal, in
all essentials. But he is not an animal, and cannot
be brought into psychological parity with one.

Confessedly, there are many limits to the freedom of both. A marked limitation to the animal is seen in the ordinance which prescribes its more feeble intellectual powers. That for man does not spring so much from an original abridgment of his faculties (for their range is practically unlimited) as from the conservative reaction of some of his advanced informations, especially his moral judgments, upon the mind itself. Man cannot and will not do many things, within easy reach of his moral powers, simply because he is a *law unto himself,* through the force and dignity of his moral conceptions. He may increase in knowledge to any extent, and increase of knowledge is increase of power. That much is granted. But power must conform to knowledge, and some knowledge is sturdily repressive in its teachings, and will determine our acts accordingly.

Remark the consequences. We fix attention upon the right or wrong of something to be done. We ought, or we ought not, to do some particular thing. We hesitate. The wheels of life move on, but there comes upon us a solemn sense of *righteous restraint,* which we cannot away with, in exchange for the less restricted liberties of animals. For indeed, though our giftlier intelligence sends us off to the school of morals, and we come away with a new power over conduct, yet because we have risen to a knowledge of the obligatory character of right, our walk and conversation must henceforth conform to the constraining pressure, and corrective discipline, of our new master.

Nevertheless, man is free, by right of informations achieved by his unique intellectual efforts. For these are in order to power. But now that, in virtue of moral informations, he has become a moral self, he is no longer free to act without them, but must go into his every act of choice in deference to such restrictive or repressive considerations as inspire his soul with a conscious responsibility for his acts. Thenceforth, his way of life is determined by moral conceptions, not by license. In exchange for unrestrained and unbridled impulses he has now the disciplinary constraint of moral truth, unfolding wide vistas of the supremacy and sovereignty of right and righteous governance.

Yes, even thought itself cannot now lead him forth into many possible and practicable ventures. It is estopped by some of the very truths it has discovered. It may still go forward discursively, and mayhap to perilous lengths, as aforetime, but every such excursion tells in the steady strengthening of judgment. And the judgment in turn will affirm and validate, with ever-increasing emphasis, the conceptions of right and wrong, duty, obligation, etc.

But this last achievement remits man to the inexorable primacy and rigorous reprisals of conscience, giving him that authoritative delimitation for conduct which builds on moral convictions.

III

My next study is the part played by mind in acquiring moral informations. I need not say that this is done by the methods of logical scrutiny and judgment.

We are now in the sphere of conscience. The actor is a unit of moral powers. And the thing done is therefore the work of a sole agency whose sovereign prerogatives are put to an interchangeable use between all the members, which, in turn, serve it in accordance with the scheme of subordination which prescribes their functions.

However, there can be no personal responsibility until the actor has consciously informed himself of the constraint, or urgency, which signalizes the authority of moral convictions. He must be informed of their awful significance. And he must affirm, or opine, that he is bound by his conceptions of right and wrong, even though he may outrage conviction by bad conduct.

The question comes up here: Whence this obligation in morals; on what does it found? Our answer is that man, as a unit of power over conduct, frames a judgment of the good or bad qualities in his acts, and conceives, or affirms, himself to be personally responsible for their commission. And this power to evalue acts as good or bad, places him in a rank to himself among terrestrial creatures. But to be more explicit: Because of his uniquely human gifts, he is constrained (as a discoverer of moral sanctions and their *stress*) to act from a conviction of his personal responsibility for their employment. For, once seeing their obligatory character, the force of the obligation is felt to be a personal motor in all that pertains to conduct.

IV

Why a conception of the moral qualities of our acts turns up a further conception, that we are personally under bonds to them, is a matter of curious interest. In other language, why does a rational witnessing of individual acts of right and wrong come back to us, as persons open to their moral pressure?

An answer might be gathered from previous discussions. We are referring to that astounding transcendence of human reason by which we alone of all God's creatures can grasp the idea of a *righteous power* seated in every moral conception. For he who discovers such knowledge, discovers its power over conduct; judging himself, and others, by what he and they do; even appraising his very thoughts by the potencies which distinguish, and emphasize, their diverse characters.

I take it that you are now aware of the estimate I put on the mind of animals. I spoke of their perspicacity being as clear as that of man, allowance being made for their narrower horizon. They reason quite knowingly, within their confined outlook. They have even ends and aims which they pursue, but they stop short of the Heaven-born distinctions, discovered and affirmed by the broader and deeper intellectual vision of man, in virtue of which distinctions, he comes to know of an austerity in moral sanctions utterly unknown to feebler intelligences. They lack power of mind to frame an articulate conception of the divine mission of right to rule in the realm of morals. And it is for this reason that moral power, as both constructive and conceptive of the equities, beauties, humanities, and duties, and culture of a human soul, is unknown to them.

But wherein lies the diversely marked superiority of man — seeing that he also is hedged in with limitations, as inviolable as those of animals? For, neither can demit one iota of what is peculiar to himself, or to itself. But man has committed to him the strictly human charge of doing right or wrong, in deference to a giftlier conception of the steps and extent of the obligation. He discovers the *meum* and *tuum* of our humanities, and in acquiring this knowledge he acquires its obligatory sanctions.

It is to be remembered, however, that, on a first acquaintance with this human *meum* and *tuum*, the mine and thine, the right and wrong of morals, etc., we see only the actions of the different actors. This alone is our first seeing.

And let me add that it is just here that the ideas of right and wrong begin to emerge in and through their concrete relations. And it occurs in this way: On one seeing himself, and others, *doing acts* involving questions of mine and thine, right and wrong, he is in the attitude of conceiving the moral character of those acts. For he remarks that they are accredited by a certain tone which claims and enforces precedence over all other actions and among all men. But the thing seen is not wholly an apprehension of right and wrong in the concrete, nor even a judgment of the moral quality of the act. It is more. A further judgment of approval or censure of the act, as intrinsically good or bad in the doer, comes in to affirm the latter's responsibility for its commission.

It is to be observed, too, that the one who sits in judgment, and approves, or reprehends, is having himself so informed of the qualities in such particulars of conduct, that he can side with, or against, them. But this is an act of choice, or the affirmation of personal preference, on evidence for it. We conclude, therefore, that when one sees, or does, an act which he conceives to be right or wrong, he is in fact adjudging himself to be a right or wrong doer; affirming choice, and, at the same time, visiting upon himself the moral reprisals of self-approval, or rebuke. For the judgment is that, inasmuch as he is the doer of the act, he is to be personally commended, or else reprehended. In either case, he is upheld by that fealty to himself, and the accepted stress of his moral convictions by which he asserts a personal preference, or sides with what he does, and so commends or eschews his own acts, as good or bad, in the light of his moral conceptions.

And ever thus, from the hour of responsibility, when one reaches a judgment of right or wrong, he is also affirming one of praise or censure (which is an affirmative or negative choice), and he is therefore also affirming his personal responsibility for choice and conduct.

For these reasons, therefore, I regard a judgment

that a given act is right or wrong for the person, as in fact one of approbation or blame; for praise or blame is the personal pairing with, or separating from, the act; choosing or eschewing it. It is choice.

V

In this connection, I may remark that, when one prefers, or sides with, or chooses, or wishes, or wills (for I use these words interchangeably), his act is indivisible and one, because he does so by all his momentum of trained faculties and aptitudes; by emotions and desires, which voice the variant powers and qualities of his thoughts; by choice, which is but the personal vehemence of the informations to which he cleaves in completing his acts.

It is apparent, therefore, that, when one does as he chooses, he goes forth as a sole potency, conceiving, and selecting, his way of life by a judgment on some alternative requirement of his own thought. But this is to work in the field of morals, and to do a work of morals is to invoke the stress of personal responsibility, and this latter is a clear departure from what obtains in simply apprehending, analyzing, and combining ordinary phenomena. For indeed, so long as we have to debate, and doubt, what to do, the specific, personal stress of final choice is unattached.

I am admitting that we may, and do, see much of conduct prospectively, and often stand face to face with the guilt or innocence which follows the fulfilment of our thoughts; forecasting thus our personal implication with the moral acts had in view. Much of this is but an exercise of discursive power, pure and simple. But until we say: I go upon my own opinion, right or wrong; I assume the sole responsibility for my every effective choice or act; until we can say this, we are not evoking the moral stringency of a judgment of right or wrong.

We see then that the soul has in it more than intellectual conceptions, pure and simple. For, to be aware only of our simply intelligent affirmations is to be simply gnostic. But to be paused in a state of moral tension, by questions which call for final action, is to catch the idea of a power in moral conceptions to bear rule in deciding all questions of right and wrong, mine and thine, equity, justice, etc. It is to be not only competently moral, but competently human, as well.

It may take a longer or shorter time to make the point of welcoming this last discovery of reason, revealing, as it does, a new aspect of choice in the constraints of a righteous law for conduct. The essential thing is faithfully to carry out its behests.

VI

But is the authority of unaided human reason our sole support for this universal sway of right? Certainly not, if indeed, as I have endeavored to show, every exterior power is so far an aid to thought that it leads it forth afield to its wider supports.

But cannot we point to some thing superior to finite thought for an obligation so intensely personal that it vehemently cries out: "Something *must* be done, and something other *must not* "?

Allow me, however, first to test the strength of a judgment of right and wrong. The subject calls for a more careful treatment than I can pretend to give it. It is not, as I have before stated, to take a careless view of an act that may be conceived to be either right or wrong. It is rather to discover, and put a value upon, the right and wrong of individual acts, and so be in a position to award and apportion merit and demerit to the respective actors.

Now, a mere casuist may make what his little pate pleases of the force of this judgment. But its one ineffaceable trait no man can disturb. As a psychological constituent, imbedded in the conception itself, it so commands our homage that it can never be divested of one iota of its peculiar stress upon our conduct.

But to return to our inquiry! As the affirmance of our own moral powers, as seen in the oughtness of our conceptions, is the subjective ground of our obligation, so a conception of divine intelligence, as our moral governor and original furnisher of moral susceptibilities, must reinforce the earlier subjective discovery.

For, when the idea of right and wrong is seen to be a fundamental and beneficent conception of One inexorably just, the obligation comes home to us, fortified and justified by divine sanctions. And further! When, by the help of this wider and diviner knowledge, we pause to estimate the practical honesties of conduct, we shall side with our judgment emotionally, with a profounder regard for what is involved in an act for which we deem ourselves personally responsible.

VII

As a further qualification and development of our contention, in respect of the march of thought into the realm of morals, I submit a few remarks upon the problem of a revelation of morals by God.

This I may not linger upon, because the Revelation itself, like everything else we witness for, can be accredited only through the evidences of moral transformations perpetually affirmed in affirming what we and others are doing and thinking when engaged in our ordinary avocations, and without which it were utterly impossible to appreciate the evidences for a Revelation.

And here, I would have the reader to pardon me for making room for sundry statements, to prevent misconception.

I am aware that all civilized and Christian peoples, nowadays, are sedulously taught of the ideas of morals by pious parents, pastors, Sunday schools, Bible classes, the catechism, etc. But whilst admitting all this, what I am contending for is that the Revelation would fail of effect, if man, or even child, lacked the capacity to remark upon, and evalue, the evidence for morals founded on what we observe of our acts. For if these acts have no moral significance to our intelligence, the Revelation could never be accredited to us. The truth is, no man can believe anything, Revelation or not, unless from his human point of view he can see abundant and overwhelming evidences of its truth. Belief must have evidence of some kind to support it. If, for instance, it were revealed to us of the nineteenth century that the sun is borne aloft in the heavens by a pair of enormous wings that propelled him through the immensities, this would be a revelation absolutely incredible, because absolutely void of any tangible evidence.

But, now, note a distinction! If, for instance, we were told by scientists that the sun sailed through the interminable spaces in quest of little pellets of fire, upon which he fed and fattened, this would be a revelation that we might, in time, be taught to accept, for reasons dimly plausible; allowance be-ing made for any poetic or literary embellishments employed in announcing such a sensational discov-ery, and remembering that science is, even now, on the lookout for the discovery of the way in which the sun keeps up, or replenishes, his fires.

So of Revelation. If any one of average intelli-gence is given a show of evidence, he will believe it, the more so, because he has a revelation of God in the flesh, as seen in the moral conceptions which he achieves. And, therefore, if it be accredited at all, it will have to lean upon that God-given reach of mental vision by which we conceive the austere sanctions of morals. For human conduct is determined by the tenor and tone of the concep-tions that enter into it.

But how fares the moral attitude of peoples who have had no revealed religion? There are many such even now. Have they no morals? Take China, for an example. Her sturdy civilization and morals have braved the ravages of time from a period anteceding the pyramids of Egypt. Who taught them morals? Who could teach them Christian morals, at any time before the days of St. Paul? But, even he confessed that the heathen were "a law unto themselves." But, if this their law was not a revelation, whence came it, except through a power of mind to conceive the "law." On the other hand, if you show me a people without morals of some kind to steady its eccentric gyrations, I will show you a mob of unintellectual wretches.

CHAPTER XII

SOME desultory remarks, growing out of previous discussions, may find place here.

1. In default of objects within reach of mind, the power of thought would fade into nothingness. Without mind, the same objects would be zero. Again, if our informations are imperfect, the power to shape conduct would be equally imperfect, if not wholly rooted out of being. For, just as we lack knowledge, we suffer a corresponding shortage in all our possibilities. Wisdom is added power. And therefore, if thought never came home to us with a distinct accession of power for combating other powers, we should be more than conditioned by those powers. We should be their slaves.

2. In these remarks, I am endeavoring to fix attention upon one or two points: —

(*a*) By an ordinance of God, there are sensations whose source of power is outside of man's initiative. And being outside, and therefore beyond our power of initiation, they interfere with our freedom no more than our bodily members interfere with it; their office being determined by a pre-arrangement of superior wisdom, for helping us into a position where we can help ourselves.

(*b*) By the same ordinance (of course, with the

help of body, sensation, environment, etc.) there is projected upon the plane of being the faculty for discursion and *personal* power, whose office it is to discover a knowledge of ourselves and our exteriorities, and thereby deal with ourselves, and things not ourselves, in view of personal responsibility for what we do.

3. When things are significant, it is their significance that appeals to mind. And for that reason, the active, curious, seeing intelligence makes opportunity of everything about it, even the most obscure and unobtrusive traits, to turn them to some advantage connected with our hopes and fears, manner and plan of life, business, etc. For the future of every one is born of the rational estimate he puts upon the significance, or meaning, hid away in the appearance and behavior of the things which confront his intelligence. And, if we could not interpret these signs, we could not employ them in mapping out, and working up to, our future.

4. It is to be noted that in all my contention, I have given sensor irritations the power to act on me dynamically, though not cognitively; whereas I have for my own part, left myself free to act cognitively and even dynamically. Now, if this be a correct psychology, cannot my thought affirm these exterior dynamics, and so get me, thus far, on the road to a more familiar acquaintance with my neighbors, and the *mine* and *thine* of our intercourse. You see, they cannot supplant my thought, though they can, and do, act *on* me. But here the reciprocity is thoroughgoing. I cannot act for, or

in the place of, my neighbors, nor they, for, or in the place of, me; but each can act upon the other. The law applies as well to one as to the other. What is permitted, and what is inhibited, involves both.

· Now then, if I can know these my neighbors, and work up to all I know of them, I may so modify their action as to fortify my own powers, and control, or modify, theirs, to my profit. In other words, I can compel them to yield me service, to the full extent of my rational discoveries.

5. We have seen matter and mind acting on each other, the former delivering a sensorial excitation, as a preliminary to the co-action of the latter's contrasting powers. And the conclusion to which I perpetually recur is that any potency, which only conditions a free cause, is but a preliminary to the latter's hold on its diverse resources, and cannot, therefore, derogate from its freedom, and for the plain reason that what is thus exterior can, by no means, usurp the prerogatives of a power whose function is ideation and discursion.

For, thought is equipped with unique and inviolable resources of its own, by virtue of which it must proceed consciously; must be attentive, and, to that extent, discursive and volitional; must be perceptive, conceptive, considerate, judicial, and, therefore, personal, self-reliant, and responsible, ere yet it can be said to be in a position to act for itself. And, if this be so, there can be no question of its freedom, for it has had its own rational way of dealing with itself, and things not itself.

But we now turn to other problems.

K

PART III

THE POWER OF INFORMATIONS

CHAPTER XIII

Introductory Remarks

In the preceding discussions, I offered some explanations of how we acquire knowledges; holding that they are conscious achievements, and, therefore, faithful products, of mind. My object now is quite different. Hereafter, I shall presume that we have been measurably stocked with knowledge, and are now casting about to see what we can do with it. "Knowledge is (personal) POWER"; and, inasmuch as, by supposition, we are now somewhat conversant with its pretensions, I feel like giving it the benefit of an experimental display of its peculiar dynamics.

It is apparent that I shall still have to do with ideas; but not now, as mere acquisitions, for I am regarding them as potencies dominating *conduct*. They are, therefore, henceforth, to be viewed as personal factors employed in consummating the work of thought in hand. It will be my aim, accordingly, to show that the real efficient in conduct is the power of knowledge, information, opinion, conception, judgment, etc.

I

You are doubtless familiar with the theory of Locke which likens mind to a sheet of blank paper written upon by sensations and foisted upon our attention. Such a crude theory effectually estops the individuality of thought, for the paper is not even sensitive. It is a blank, simply and sheerly passive and receptive. It has no activity which is distinctly its own. It can neither know a sensation, nor define its functions and connectives. It has no way of acquiring knowledge.

But let the paper theory pass. Locke would deny much of all this. But Locke is inconsequent, vacillating, inconsistent, and could not accomplish the impossible. His theory is a failure. We cannot delay upon it.

However, my immediate task is to show that it is misleading, in that it dwells upon what is delivered to thought, and not on what thought *does*. I shall presently make this point.

Nevertheless, it is noteworthy that the office of thought has been a mystery on which writers have offered many a brave conjecture, without clearing up the mystery. But, now that we begin to make some steady progress in the remorseless capture of facts, the mystery may subside as the facts accumulate.

II

Availing myself of these recent advances, I may venture to pronounce a theory more in keeping with the power of thought, as a discursive energy competent for its appointed work.

Locke summoned us to note the power of sensations in furnishing thought with something for its study. In a spirit of liberality, I may presume this to be Locke's view. And it is correct, when relieved of its one-sidedness. On the contrary, and in order to clear up the problem, I would, in contrast, dwell upon what thought does as a discursive energy working upon things not itself, but ever with the intention of promoting some interest personal to itself.

My theory is exemplified by the spectacle of little children playing in my front yard. Snow is falling fast and furious, and they are sporting in its fleecy folds, delightedly imbibing the joy of childish power, spite of struggles with the warring elements. For the chubbiest cheek among them has the courage of his infantile convictions, and welcomes the fray with the enthusiasm of a would-be Roman gladiator.

The reader may contrast this picture with that of Locke. And it might be helpful, in this connection, to bear in mind that I began my lucubrations with a little nursling of the cradle. It will be remembered that we saw it battling with environment, conditions, etc., inner and outer, innumerable. For we allowed these exteriorities the full benefit of their offensive, but limited dynamics. And now, it is only fair that we should be as liberal with our child, giving it, likewise, an opportunity for a display of its counter-activities. Every power acting on the child was greeted with the kindest appreciations. And we explained how the youngster gladly caught up knowledge, and waxed stronger. For getting knowledge is getting *personal* power. And now, it behooves us frankly to acknowledge this power, — seen in children, and seen in men. And yet children and men are so very, very finite that they cannot act in disregard of the objects which act on them. So of all things exterior; for these also are similarly conditioned by the objects that act on them.

I have heretofore remarked upon all this. For child or man, or animal or thing, or "principalities or powers," or things present and to come, are bound by the fundamental laws for their being and interactions. They did not come of a sudden without roots extending away back to some original thought in God. I have likewise offered an explanation of how all these exteriorities contributed to unfold the slumbering intelligence of our little folk, giving it place as a power uniquely personal by reason of its preëminent moral, discursive, and progressive traits.

Children have all these distinctively human traits, then!

Otherwise, to revert to my illustration, whence comes this sportive tilt of mind and muscle with the pitiless forces of nature? Is it not the veritable stepping forth of a counter-activity with resources other than material and naturalistic; even a conscious, eager, thoughtful energy that makes conquest, as it cultivates the powers of thought? Mind can have no life and no activity except as it knows. For, when it is once known that nature is governed by laws so tempered that our finite intelligence can discover their meaning, and employ this knowledge in furthering our personal ends, then, the joy of triumph may leap from our hearts, as we go forth to battle in the might of our convictions.

III

The inquiry to which I devote the present discussion may be subdivided into chapters, in accordance with the general plan marked out for resolving all knowledge into the questions of *power* which it includes.

But I am not to be understood as attempting to draw the line between the different provinces of knowledge with entire accuracy. It is sufficient for my purpose to take up in order such as will measurably present the fact of power in knowledge. I premise, therefore, with some needed distinctions.

Informations may be divided into two general classes, as follows: —

1. Those which give us facts in concrete or individual presentations, after the manner of the child's first visual apprehension of an object, when we have the result of an off-hand, first acquaintance with the object. These may be termed the strictly *perceptive* informations. They will not, however, be separately dwelt upon in what follows, chiefly because they but hold up before the mind the different objects so affirmed for closer study and elaboration, in order to a better knowledge of their significance for our discursive purposes.

2. The other class is born of that much more reconstructive power of mind which discovers and

coördinates the parts or attributes which constitute a concrete object, or objects, as we are enabled to conceive and affirm them and their kindred affiliations, or the mutual dependence subsisting between a group of different objects interacting under the law for their social intercourse.

I need scarcely repeat that all such informations are worked up from the things of self and its exteriorities, and carefully compared, in order to strengthen and extend our own powers, every item of which tends to increase our personal or individual powers; for such conceptions enable us to act for ourselves, and hence are prized according to their efficiency in accomplishing our purposes. They are our true conceptions, or informations, being discursive, constructive, and efficient in conduct. And here truth is valued, not so much as an isolated idea, good for its spectacular significance, but as a something we would carefully inquire into and work up into its distinctive relations to ourselves and other things from which we would wrest some secret of power, or advantage to ourselves.

Now, it is this last class I am proposing to consider; and it is divided into two subordinate ones: —

(1) Preparatory Informations.

(2) Actile or Ultimating Informations.

I am not now concerned with describing the mere facts of conception, proper to either class. My main object is to call attention to, and to emphasize, the *power* of knowledge remarked in our acts, giving us the operative and finalizing aspect of knowledge.

One more remark! Mind is equally active, efficient, and constructive, whether engaged in acquiring, or utilizing knowledge. For every conception is born of the constructive exploitations that achieve it. It is nevertheless true that the mind's acquisitions are one thing, and the ultimating stress of such acquisitions in actualizing the purposes and plans of life, is another thing.

CHAPTER XIV

Preparatory Informations

Heretofore I have been engaged in the study of informations, but not as yet concluding what to do with them. What I propose now is to regard them as discoveries or achievements, standing before conduct as a ready, or else expectant, impulsion or cause exercising a directive, controlling, or decisive *power* over conduct.

I

I explain briefly. All knowledge is obtained through the metamorphic scrutiny of attention and affirmation, on evidence. We observe and distinguish parts in an ensemble of contents, *i.e.*, judge on evidence. And this process is resorted to, it may be, with a blushing and halting anticipation of clearer results, even when we are demarking our first ideas; a subsequent and more subtle elaboration bringing in discursive informations or proper rational discoveries. For mind, even at the very beginning of its career, must inspect the instreaming of exterior (or even interior) impressions in order to construct ideas of them.

II

But what concerns us now are such informations as are framed in view of some ulterior result, and, for that reason, are both constructive and prospective. Here, the soul is not only inquisitive and acquisitive, but a pronounced power of innovation, preparing for a work of thought. It will, therefore, have to ascertain the practical limits of its own, and other powers, and measure the participation of each in a result still in the future, and so be in a position to make use of such discoveries as may open the way to complete a work that promises some conceived advantage to itself. And here, too, it must ascertain what it can do, and also what it prefers doing; and it must, most literally, acquire this knowledge, ere it can ever become intelligently active and directive.

I am proceeding cautiously. For I have to construct my way as I advance, *in tenebras, in ignotum.*

We are, as I said, about to apply our knowledges; employing them as powers going into deeds for which we are responsible. But this cannot be done in disregard of what we conceive to be conducive to our good. We shall, hence, be preparing to do a contemplated work, for some reason intensely human and personal. The logic of enlightened self-interest and self-protection is to *know* and *do.* And, therefore, we keep a sharp lookout for our interests, seeking such informations as we may need when we come to act.

Observe that we have now reached a stage in our psychological pilgrimage where we begin to project desires, hopes, fears, joys, purposes, etc., bearing upon our happiness, and to ask ourselves whether we are, or are not, so conversant with our own and other powers that we can secure a limited control of the latter, to our own betterment.

But all the aforementioned informations are an accumulation of so much personal power in prospect of actual fruition. They pertain to the future, and bring under review a multitude of things thought to be promotive of our happiness and which we may not ignore without palpable stultification. And if we do not propose to utilize them in the present, it is because we are judiciously reserved until the day for final action. More tersely put, I may say: We have been prosecuting our inquiries in prospect of appeasing our cultivated wants and would act even as we know.

Our problem is, therefore, a question of the power of knowledge, and how to employ it decisively in the acts of a soul alive to intelligent and moral requirements. And we shall have to compare our powers with those of our surroundings, and to decide what we shall do with ourselves, and what with our surroundings.

The object of pursuit is not now in existence and ripe to our contemplation; but we must open a way for doing a work of the future that, on its completion, will evidence the power of our thoughts. And if we do that work, we give the world a new something which had no existence until our thought went forth to establish it, — for our praise or blame. It is in this way, and with this intent, that we canvass and solve every problem of life.

And here again we see that knowledge is personal power; the power of *our* ideas.

Proceeding further with our analysis, we note another distinction.

As our intellectual powers expand, we become more intelligently inquisitive. Our native propensity for knowledge may be satisfied with the mere acquisition of knowledge. But once having it in hand, we have its power, and in turn become more intelligently and definitely anxious to test its practical possibilities, and so we begin to rate things as useful, æsthetic, good, or bad, etc., in respect of ourselves and others; and the ever-springing sanguineness that comes from repeated triumphs of thought prompts us to make preliminary investigations bearing on the object had in view.

But not until we are in charge of our rational guides can we venture to realize any just expectation. Meantime, we have been weighing the facts, in order to determine their relative value for getting within reach of our object.

III

In practice, the process resorted to is partly remembrance and comparison, but, preëminently, it is a preliminary wrangle for a working theory involving the exercise of constructive powers, whereby the potencies of things about us are retouched with the elastic transformations of mind, and so brought to display a range of power denied to their unaided nature.

For instance, here is something still in the future. It will take years of thought and muscle to work it up. For it cannot be realized, now and here. But, as it is in the line of expectancy and hopefulness, we make a vigorous effort to consummate our purposes. And it is so that, by the steady painstaking of thought, it is brought, nearer and nearer, to completion. By and by, it is a finished product of reason. It is now realized, and in position, as a veritable creation; a new something, and ours, by virtue of the power of our thought.

A fact like the following is not an unusual occurrence: A number of farmers are thinking of establishing a bank with a capital of one hundred thousand dollars. One hundred farmers agree to contribute; each one thousand dollars. But where is the money to come from, seeing they have none in hand? They resolve to go home and work for it, laying by their surplus earnings annually. At the expiration of four or five years each is ready with the contribution agreed upon, and the bank is established and officered. Here is a new creation that, a few years agone, had no existence whatever. But it confronts us now, a brave commercial structure which for years hung on the constructive and prospective informations of its projectors.

But now the same farmers would build a road. And how is this to be done? They put their heads together and conclude upon its feasibility, prospectively plan its execution, and ultimately build it as planned.

The same plan is adopted whenever the ubiquitous railroad calls for money. And I might make mention of divers other monuments of constructive thought, such as churches, temples, art museums, etc., conceived and determined upon by a consideration of the moral and æsthetic aspirations of cultivated peoples.

I select these facts of every day's observation, in order to bring out the point, that the power of informations prepares the way for our attacking all the problems of life and business. For every information is just so much mental power, and every effort made is a tactful, careful, constructive move of thought toward a result not yet reached.

The field of man's work is committed to himself. It rests upon him, therefore, to acquire the requisite pupillary knowledge, ere he would take the plunge into business. If he seek his own good, he must inform himself, and labor to possess it. He must know of his wants and wishes, and strive to realize them. His chief concern is himself, and what pertains to his welfare. And yet, if he would make sure of his own good, he will have to allow for what is not himself.

All knowledge has an emphasis pointing to conduct, and we have to await the day when, after much thought, we can reach conclusions on which to act. We see that some things can be entreated to confer a good; some, a beauty, and other some, a utility. And we like the flavor of this discovery and plan to possess them. We have a boundless field for exploration wherein to get knowledge and qualify ourselves for compassing our ends. This is but to get ready for work and look forward to

L

its accomplishment; appreciating our discoveries as instrumental to the object in view.

In any event, and in respect of any proposed work, we must see and interpret certain traits in the things we are contemplating which promise points applicable to the problem before us, and then aligning cause and effect with the direction of our purposes, conclude upon a course of conduct that will secure our object.

This will be apparent in what follows. We may be conversant with corn, as merchandise. But now we wish to grow it. Here it behooves us to be prospective, constructive, and practical. It is a question of bread, and a living competency. So, we must satisfy ourselves that the land is productive, and that we have the means for its cultivation. And, therefore, the question of labor is considered: horses and men; their hire and board; and whether they are trustworthy, tractable, serviceable, etc. And, if we are satisfied on these points, our prospection is completed, and we go to work.

But wherein consists the peculiarity of such informations? Only in this: They are *rational powers held in reserve for the future.* They mean business, but, for the present, it is only a proposed venture requiring special thought. Think of it! The farmer has to control himself, lest he act prematurely. He must have command of natural forces, and bend them to his purposes. But in order to this, he must know them with a knowledge so searching that he can discern the supreme correlations existing between things individual, but capable of co-acting, if needed in furthering a contemplated result. In other words, he must shape his way to acts through the special considerations that go to establish them.

IV

I foresee that my account of preparatory informations will be imperfect, unless I allow for their effect in qualifying the mind itself for its peculiar work. A brief exposition of this must suffice.

Every accession of such knowledge adds to the mind's efficiency; for every efficiency is born of the mind in its proximate antecedent condition, and so carried over into the new birth. Hence comes the fact that all our informations become in time a psychological investment looking forward to conduct, and finally reappearing there as the result of our previous thoughts.

For whilst thought is being trained, it is accumulating a fund of prospective informations which are intrenched in the faculties, and held over for future exigencies; acquisitions of the past reappearing as expert efficiencies of the present. Indeed, if we have knowledge through an intelligent appreciation of facts, we must found on our previous acquisitions and present dexterity; every succeeding information being dependent on the view the mind can then take of its then wants. Wherefore, as we grow in knowledge, we augment the reserves of information which continue with the soul as trained, or educated, efficiencies subject to our call.

And yet, it is still true, that when we would do something new, we shall have to reform our outlook, somewhat. For we have to discover, and consider, not alone how to make use of our present acquisitions, be they what they may, but how to meet wants which are just now responding to our sharpened apperceptions.

CHAPTER XV

IN the matter of actively employing our rational faculties, much of their character is brought out on a limited experience and observation of the reasons why we act at all. I am now referring to the beginnings of our experience. For instance, we are meditating a possible, or probable, act to be done *in futuro*. Inquire now, why are we contemplating such an act. The answer is: We have *reasons* for it. In this way it will be seen that we have a reason for pondering any future act.

I

But now, if we regard man as an actor going beyond his preparatory lucubrations into performance, we find that he takes this last step also,—because he has reasons for it. He has had, we may say, a *minimum* of experience of the first kind, and this may be a reason why he would know something of the power forward of his purely subjective, but preparatory, reasons or contemplations; the fact of his being finite affording a sufficient reason why he should try to discover the extent of both his own and other powers. At all events, the efficiency in both kinds of informations is a controlling reason.

149

And similarly a controlling reason, good or bad, determines his willingness to do anything. Yea, even as his mind has been schooled to value good or bad acts, so will it have a corresponding sequence of acts. For what is a responsible or personal act must ever answer to the power of some foregoing opinion; man being an actor solely by virtue of the power of his thoughts. Indeed, every act of man has an individual character which rests on the different kind of informations that inform it. And hence, we are driven to the conclusion that we can neither begin, nor continue, a train of reasoning, nor give effect to any thought, in any way, without this controlling efficiency of our every thought.

II

Having done with the above preliminary explanations, I hope we are now prepared for considering the problem of *actile* or *ultimating* informations, more distinctly. It is to be remarked that every information, on reaching its final stage, has passed beyond the condition of a mere subjective acquisition, and pushed its way to a final term. For, when it begets a completed work, it has assumed that last change which a knowledge of the approved time and place, and other finalizing touches of action, determines. It becomes an operating power in what we do, then and there.

But this last phase, too, is a question of one's reasons, or desires, or choice; and it ultimates, either one or the other, as we may choose to regard them.

For, as will hereafter be explained, one cannot do an act without desiring to do it, nor desire to do it without some reason or motive for the desire; nor indeed do it in any way at all without choice, which is simply the final stage of our operative or actile thought, or reason, or desire.   And, therefore, our desire to do it is some reason or motive, ending in preference or choice, which is the ultimate term or decisive phase of our reason for doing it.   Choice is reason, or motive, ultimated.

I remark, further, that if we ultimate, or give the final tone to an idea or information, we do it on choice, and choice is the actile power in a given information which decides our personal preference and responsibility.   So then, to ultimate the information is to give it our personal adherence in act, which is preference or choice.   But this is to liberate its actile or finalizing power.   And, therefore, when we say we are responsible for our opinions, we mean that we have given them the last touch of final approval or choice.

III

Glancing for a moment at the moral aspects of the problem, we are to consider such informations as urge us with an authority intensely stringent. And now, if we ultimate these last, we have gone upon an act of responsible choice which expresses the sovereign power of moral convictions.

But why are these so urgent?

Because having, once for all, adventured their discovery, we have uncovered an element of vehe-

mence in them, presented, it may be, more tensely,
but not more indisputably, than that of any of our
ordinary informations.   For every information has
an actile vehemence of its own, which qualitatively
distinguishes it from all others.   And now, if we
are to act on these, we must have the light of other
informations, to determine the question of acting,
then and *there*.   And therefore, again, the reason
for coming to an act of choice is some ancillary
information with power to precipitate and ultimate
the force of the main one.   And I may add that,
as the urgency in moral, or for that matter, in any
other conceptions, is itself a discovery of thought,
it will be acted on, finally or not, just as the mind
has been trained to prize it in comparison with such
as found on slighter considerations.

IV

I have, before, explained that thought lives by
knowing; acquiring mental power, and utilizing this
power, in its own way, and for good and sufficient
reasons.   I have also pointed out that ultimating
informations and desires are but different aspects of
the same thing.   For the latter are present and ultimated, in every act of choice, because they do but
express the emotional or personal phase of the ultimating information (or reason).

Inasmuch, then, as desires represent the omnivo-
rous gatherings of thought, they perform the office
of furnishing us with a provisional orientation upon
which we may act, on choice or preference.   And,
therefore, if thought does gather up all knowledges

and give them the aforementioned, provisional orientation, as seen in our desires, all we have to do, when we go upon some final act or procedure, is either to act with such desires as we may then prefer, or else cast out these, and act on such as we can espouse from a different point of view.

It may be objected, however, that desires often exercise a very notable *pressure* on thought and conduct. This we have no reason to deny, especially in view of the fact that the desires themselves, with their quantity and quality of impelling force, have been mediated *by the mind*, and the pressure is consequently intelligent and voluntary, and that we are supporting both desires and their pressure by a rational estimate of the suitability of the objects desired to our condition and circumstances. The pressure is of our own procurement and so must bespeak our mind.

For whenever we come to an act of choosing or preferring, or fulfilling a given desire, we shall be found desiring something intensely, or, *vice versa,* languidly, just as we are informed of and value the urgency at the instant of preference.

So, too, we may desire, or choose, or prefer, frivolously, because our informations (and consequently, our appreciation) of the urgency are not serious; or indifferently, because they are not satisfactory; or even stupidly, because they are inadequate, etc. And here, again, it is evident that the so-called pressure or urgency of desires lies in the force of our convictions, and that both responsible choice and fulfilled desire express that force.

The Gulf Stream is impelled by the heat of the sun. But here is a psychological stream of desires propelled by the fervor of rational convictions and evaluations; a fervor, let me repeat, which is awakened, and continued in being, solely by the power of thought.

V

A few words about desires finally rejected may be allowed in this place.

The *ipse dixit* of thought has aforetime stored these with their measure and degree of preparative, or provisional, choice. But whether they be chosen and acted upon is left to some finalizing thought or opinion.

A similar exposition applies to motives. For what are they but the soul's rational hold on what it can choose or finally desire? Or, we may preferably define them as desires looked at as a rational, or moral, impulsion or personal fervor, with a clear purgation of unthinking animalism.

So also of inducements. These are indifferently rational impulsions or rational desires, either subjective or objective; the first looking within upon the intent; the latter regarding, more particularly, the reasons drawn from the *object* concerning which we are taking an interest, — reasons why it should be prized or valued as ancillary to the true purpose within. In either case, the determination issues from the intent or purpose, or, if you prefer, the desire or personal potency found in the final *thought.*

And, therefore, in this regard, an objective inducement is in fact a subjective desire, motive, or purpose. In other words, we may view the power of an objective inducement as that of a conception in order to rational action, our every act being determined by a subjective cause, or the power of some final thought conditioned on the quality of mind we have on hand, as the result of the opportunities we have improved. But these points will receive fuller explication in subsequent discussions.

CHAPTER XVI

POWERS IN AID OF FREE DETERMINATIONS

THIS chapter is not intended as a mere summary of previous discussions. The powers under consideration are all such as, when correctly understood, may be taken to be for an *aid* to thought, volition, or free determinations. They, indeed, operate on thought, in special ways, but are not its volitional powers.

I

I begin with the Appetencies. I may describe them as native impulsions, born with the child. As such, they present themselves as sensorial visitations, ere yet the child has come into the possession of any idea, emotion, desire, or knowledge of any kind, unless I except a confused cognition of their simultaneous irruption upon its attention, at the instant of birth. And, therefore, is the child startled, as I have said, by the presence of such unbidden and unheralded strangers, at such a time.

I shall speak very guardedly of this dark delta that begirts the infant soul. Meantime, let us await disclosures. The desire centre is not slow to manifest itself, in response to some discovery of the rational. For the rational is never off duty from

the beginning.   The moral enters the lists, later on.
At the moment of birth, there is small chance to
accentuate definite thought and action; and for a
brief interval, thought must have a herculean task
to clutch its first full idea.   The situation is embarrassing.   Here is life full of blind impulsions,
and here, too, is thought without its first articulate
idea, and only ready for its discovery.

Facts will testify of the result.   There is something in the sudden fission from the fœtal state
of the child to its separate life in the outer world,
something in the first freshness of its animal impulsions, something, too, in its tender openness to
unwonted visitations — but more in God's law for all
these infantile experiences.   But the child breathes.
Its separate life is revealing itself, and, with life,
the centre for appetencies is born unto a state of
agnostic sensation and impulsion.

And now, the question comes up, how can the
child pass these adamantine barriers ?   Can it ever
get beyond its blind gropings ?   For, as native
instigations, and therefore, blindly active and impulsive, the mission of the appetencies is not then
known, and cannot then be known, until thought
mediates between them and their, then, unknown
objects, testifying, thus, to their ancillary or auxiliary office, in respect of its own cognitive functions.

II

The office of Native Dispositions may now be
considered.   These also are original furnishings in
aid of thought and personal responsibility.   They

constitute what is peculiar in the tone and temper —the bias, mental and moral, of men, as individuals, and so distinguish one man from another. The same remarks apply to man's physique, as part of his original endowment. But now, what shall be said of this formidable array of native powers, and their bearing on thought, or volition? We answer: They are simply and solely a *subjective environment*, which does for man, after the manner of external conditions; like those, for instance, which differentiate the Chinese, or Polynesians, from Teutons, or Caucasians, whereby we have distinct groups of peoples and individuals; each with a destiny which smells of his locality and surroundings.

As original, our native dispositions are involuntary to us. And as manifested in the active details of life, some regard them as equally involuntary there.

I have, once before, demurred to this last view, by explaining that our entire, original stock of competencies, so far as and *when* they affect *conduct*, are under the strictest supervision of thought, and thus become intelligent motors whose objectives await the discovery and appraisement of the latter. For if we grant them the full force of an animal impulse, they would still lack the power to make us act blindly, when we would act deliberately and knowingly. But when we employ them, on the morrow of adult responsibility, all such as we have any reason for entreating hospitably are as voluntary as a discriminating apperception can make them, in exercising its right of choice and sanction.

So then, if we hold them to be involuntary, when manifested as modifiers of character and habits, they are to be regarded as goods in stock, like environment, conditions, the potter's clay, etc.; the voluntary efficiency having a like power over them, in some way consistent with its free determinations and distinctions.

III

As coming within the scope of my present inquiry, I mention some natural states of the body, such as vitality, power and its opposite, health and its opposite; the two latter opening the way for a feeling of unrest, or vague, disquieting apprehensions, etc., etc. For the most part, these are not so clamorous in their primitive demands as to require any particular statements. Indeed, they partake more of the character of sensations than appetencies. Nevertheless, I regard them as contributing a quite perceptible, native efficiency coming in before an act of thought, as auxiliary to its peculiar transformations. But, being a part of the constitutive outfit of thought, and therefore dating prior to, or else contemporary with, its discursions, they are in no condition to antagonize its volitional determinations, but only provide a way for their advent and subsequent behavior.

IV

Here, now, are some impulses much more importunate than simple states of either body or mind. Such are hunger, thirst, etc., — the true appeten-

cies. Any exposition of such power as may be
viewed as auxiliary to those of thought, would
be strangely imperfect, if these most importunate
motors were omitted.

We have seen that thought is a watchful energy
whose office it is to discover knowledge, and so
have the advantage of its own rôle of action in the
midst of other powers, — co-acting with, or else
modifying them, for reasons of policy, choice, etc.
Now, here are appetencies placed so near to thought
that they are in, and of, us. For body and mind
are mates from birth; and because of this intimate
union, we have a home acquaintance of mental and
moral, physical and material, modes of being and
action.

Hence our sufficiency, from early childhood, for
achieving informations and emotions which are
ours, as the unit of body and spirit, and which furnish us with the voluntary impulsions which arise
from, and express, the power of our knowledges.

As thus furnished, there can be no doubt what
we shall do when confronted with the appetencies.
We hunger and thirst, etc., but not without
the careful inquisition and coöperation of mind.
They are seen to be unthinking and blind; and
whilst attesting this, their involuntary character,
mind is contrasting itself as voluntary, with what
is involuntary in them. And now, we may discern
that the part played by all these involuntary impulsions is that of a blind, incognitive stimulation, vital,
animal, and even brutish, etc. And I may say of
them, what I said of sensations, that whatever else

they may do, they cannot usurp the *peculium* of thought, by making over to it the gift of a single rational idea, or information, of any kind. Thought remains stubbornly cognitive.

For the office of the latter, in respect of these outside forces, is to determine what manner of things they are, to discover their outlying objectives, and to appraise their value for maturing refined (here personal) impulsions, or true desires. It will, and can, act only as it is informed; and let an appetency be what it may, thought will have recourse to some exigent discursion, or perish. Wherefore if on a study of such native impulsions, mind should explicate rational impulsions, all we need say is that thought is *facile princeps*, an expert explorer, and has a right to such discoveries of its own as will give it a rational, and therefore personal, impulsion, be it emotion or desire.

Such being my views, I must hold that, whilst hunger, thirst, etc., are placed outside of mind, as native forces, the mind, for its part, constructs ideas of them and their mission, and leads them out into the ways and opportunities of intelligent impulsions, through the sweeping metamorphosis of inference and judgment.

V

Here I venture a passing remark. It will be observed that I have not spoken of these appetencies as entitled to the name of native *desires* or *emotions*. My reason is that neither the one nor the other is *native* to us, and I never meet with these

M

phrases without revolting at the inaccuracy. Appetencies are native to us, but desires and emotions are not. It is plain that one cannot desire, or be emotioned at any object, before he apprehends it. It is equally plain that there cannot be an object, for any appetency, until it is sought out and pointed out by mind. Only when thus discovered and mediated by mind can it ever be such an object. It is a better psychology which describes them as native appetencies, propensities, or predispositions, acting as blind instigations. For we are but enouncing an immovable fact, when we affirm that they depend on some propædeutic teachings of mind to reach even their most proximate objects of gratification, and yet it is a matter of much importance to have a distinct conception of what they do in aid of mind. And this shall be our next problem.

VI

In man the vital or animal impulses are under the guardianship of a rational power which conceives human events and their gratifications. He has appetencies, or propensities, which vaguely and blindly foretoken the emotions and desires which come to birth upon a conception of our intelligent wants. Ever through life, he employs the disciplinary stress and efficiency of some thought to curb or modify, or else assist or adapt, his animal impulsions. For whatever they are, and whatever they can do, he will, for his part, walk in the ways of thought. He is to them what the shepherd is to his sheep: "He putteth forth his own sheep . . . and the sheep *follow him*, for they know his voice."

This is correct and beautiful. But wherefore does he put them forth? Let us hope we can divine the reason! It is *because* there is in the sheep that which provokes him to take them in charge, and minister to their blind cravings. But he could not do this, if he could not discern those blind cravings, and, discerning them, evolve and devise a way for their gratification.

Now, this is literally the case as between man and the blind powers within him. He has to give them sight and lead them forth, providing for them the distinct opportunities revealed by his mighty discursive energy.

But here we encounter a wish for fuller explanation. The situation is about this: A mere child may be at the mercy of blind impulsions; but, as he grows older, we see him doing for them after the manner of his maturer, human type of mind. So far we are secure. And yet there is in these blind impulsions something apart from what man can do with them. This also should be allowed for. We have already given these native impulsions the office of blind instigations to thought. But now, more precisely, what is their special office in respect of the essential competencies of thought, as a discoverer of their functions? Plainly, they are intended to *orient* the beginner with some dark intimations of the sequence between an animal impulse and its satisfying objects, and so lead him to ponder, and ulti-

mately discover, their connection with his personal
and responsible wants and voluntary impulsions.

And this is the commencement of the distinctively
discursive exploits of thought, and, as you see, due
allowance has been made for the parts played both
by voluntary and involuntary forces.

I need scarcely mention the fact that this orientation discovered in the appetencies is some aspect of
divine thought seen in all His works, whether they
be statics, dynamics, attributes, relations, or aught
else, and seen there because of His law of rational
order which appeals to our intelligence.

VII

But perhaps I should explain more explicitly
what I mean by *orienting the beginner*. Well, we
are thinking of a beginner who has to discover his
facts by dint of careful scrutiny, and carry them
forward into a field of transformations denied to
impulsions strictly native and involuntary.

Now for the orientation. I have just now named
a feature in the appetencies which sets them apart
from what we can do with them. They *mean* something, and can do something *significant*. This, then,
is their orientation, and it enables thought to remark
upon, and know what to do with them and with
itself, as now instructed by what it has discovered.

And as to their meaning. Sensations, impulses,
states of mind and body, etc., yea, everything in
the universe of thought and matter, each has its
allotted complement of meanings which one may
inquire into and act upon. And so far as these

meanings can be wrested from the objects studied, they amount to a very important orientation; significant, tangible, potent, fruitful.

But, as man can neither create these potencies, nor fledge them with meaning, his task is to discover that meaning, and pursue a line of conduct corresponding with the knowledge evoked.

VIII

I have been all along admitting that our native endowments and co-acting familiars of every kind, are an indispensable aid to our voluntary determinations. Now, so far as mind is thus dependent on them for aid, the question arises, does not this dependence imply some infringement of the prerogatives of a free or volitional power?

Here it is needful to remember that any freedom we may have (and that is all we contend for) is finite, and must, therefore, depend on such limitations as restrict it to the finite. We are finite, but it is a fact, equally well pronounced, that everything that acts on us is likewise finite; even so finite that it cannot deliver a sensation, neither make any the least impression on us *without our help*, poor as it may be. As at present constituted, it is certainly something to help man, if only he have sense enough to help himself.

The Omniscient has given him veracious standards for his guidance in all this matter of potencies within and without, their help, orientation, etc.; and the more he studies them, the more he develops his several ability to command his own resources, and if so be he help himself, is not that something to his credit?

We work a crop of corn, and the land in turn kindly helps us. So much for the help of a friendly power! But does that oust us of the work we do ourselves? We opine not.

I pass on to another point closely allied to the above, but previously touched upon. Are not hunger and thirst, mental and physical states, etc., not to mention sensations, compulsory? Dare we neglect them?

I concede, at once, that all these involuntary factors have a dynamic character so forcible that I cannot refuse them due attention. Indeed, they oftenest intrude upon my thought, not seldom violently, and may destroy me at any moment. (But this latter is a question apart from the present exposition.)

It may be observed however, that by as much as they are destroying me, they are destroying themselves. "A house divided against itself cannot stand."

Still, so long as I am not totally destroyed, my voluntary efficiencies are not estopped. I have simply a very painful feature of the social dynamics of my co-acting familiars to take note of and act upon.

However, if any normal visitation from these involuntary impulsions does but allow me an opportunity to exercise my own powers, it will be readily seen that, so far from being a serious infraction of my freedom, it simply calls me to a different assertion of my discursive powers.

If my freedom has been rudely assailed, it may be abridged, to that extent, but its repair, and possible reëstablishment, may still be accorded me.

Apart from this, and under any ordinary circumstances of health and surroundings, thought cannot be got to complain of any amount of so-called *forcing* on the part of involuntary factors, either to get it into position, or to maintain it there, as a free cause sufficient for its appointed tasks.

Wherefore, from every point of view, we may regard thought as in charge of all these native forces, opening their eyes and adjusting their orientation to our dominant personal outlook, appraising and then requiting their blind importunities. It has discovered the underlying sympathy between native impulsions and those which spring from mind and morals. It has ascertained that the former are an ordained support to the latter, in that they can be transformed into intelligent and personal motors. For, emerging as purely vital motors, they are transformed into the trained efficiencies of the governing intellect, and so become our familiar desires and emotions. The result is that, having once compassed the meaning and mission of our appetencies, we begin to see some strong personal reasons for effecting that cognitive transformation which commutes what is an animal craving into an emotion, or desire, for something we conceive to be promotive of our good.

And here let me explain that, in every such transmutation, the interest manifested is to be seen in our desires and emotions, but this desire or emotion is, after all, nothing in the world but the personal or partisan interest seen in every achievement of thought. It is an element, or phase of, and born with, all knowledge.

Moreover, this personal or partisan interest, this emotion or desire, is the actual substitute for the aforetime state of appetency seen in our native impulsions. Hence, when we have once for all acquired some knowledge, we can never commit the psychological inadvertency of losing an interest in it. For knowledge is personal power, as manifested in emotions and desires. But more of this anon.

IX

When one is told of instincts coming forward in aid of thought, he is at a loss what to say or think; so little is known and so much is made of them. They are stifled under a ban which forbids their entering the current of thought. Still, I have an opinion under advisement.

Of course every faculty of the soul has its first send-off spontaneously, ere yet the intelligence is born, and in order to its birth. But, onward from that time, we have to achieve all knowledge by a rational study of phenomena. And yet, there is sometimes an appearance of acting too quickly for any rational elaboration of the matter in hand. And this has some little show of support, when we are taken by a sharp surprise which may, in part, break up the rational processes. For, if these are quite broken up, the common catastrophe would overwhelm instinct and intellect alike. I confess to some sharp surprises myself, but I never once relapsed into a condition of mind which did not allow room for the play of, at least, a hasty consideration of the situation. I may be caught up so suddenly that the suddenness of the situation will awaken thought, and with it, the corresponding emotions of fear, alarm, surprise, etc. It is to be remembered that quite a large part of the life of thought consists in knowing things by a mere glance of recognition, — thought becoming an expert, after a varied experience of cognitive marks and their evidence. But surely this is not to know them without cognitive marks, as it would be in the case of a supposed instinctive apprehension. We have no instinctive, that is to say, *unthinktive* (?) knowledges (so to speak). The act of cognition may be quite as quick as that of the supposed instinct. But what is known is a thing of evidence and judgment; an act of the thinking and judging soul.

As was said, it was needful to begin life instinctively, or, I prefer saying, *spontaneously*, before ever we had been in a condition to turn the metamorphic power of thought upon the evidences for our acts, or upon the blind intimations seen in our native impulsions. But so soon as we become discursive, that swiftest recourse of reason (misnamed instinct) is born of oft-repeated thoughts and judgments, and has its place, for reasons of economy and dispatch, in our elaborating processes; a ceaseless repetition of the more deliberate trains of reasoning, under all circumstances, ending in disastrous obstruction, as a little reflection will distinctly disclose.

You remember the protracted, difficult, and tedious processes the child resorted to in the effort to conceive the rose, the cherry, the nurse, the father, mother, and other domestic familiars, and how, having undergone this careful home-schooling, it set off to explore the universe, and perceived and conceived the horse, the landscape, cause and effect, law and order, and even God. But once completed, we may never repeat the same discursions, except under pressure of circumstances which will justify us. We abridge the toil of repeating the discursion.

And now, that we have completed the details of conception, we may, and do, neglect them, and so behold the horse, the landscape, the rose, the cherry, etc., *directly* (I say not instinctively), — that is to say, we *perceive* these objects in the mass. So that it comes to this: If, when looking at the horse, nurse, rose, etc. (after our previous elaboration of their content of attributes), we only perceive, that is, see them *directly*, it is because we keep all previous elaboration out of our eyes, or, at least, in the background, and see them immediately.

And in this sense, and for above reasons, we may be said to see even cause, law, order, and God, by a direct and immediate vision; *i.e.*, perceive them.

At all events, we can reason fast or slow, to suit the occasion and the degree of mental culture reached, and still have no need to excogitate a recrudescence like the so-called instinct of a child on the threshold of intelligence. And yet, some evolutionists can see nothing in all this manifestation of mind but " nature," " natural selection," and even "reflex action," etc.; and put it to selecting objects in advance of their presentation for selection, by way of solving a postulated mystery involved in accounting for the origin of new forms of life.

X

But, if it can be known that there is as little need for instinct in animals as in man, then it would be worse than absurd to contend for it at all. For, not many years agone, the text-books on comparative psychology assumed that animals acted on instinct alone. Nowadays, however, most philosophers recognize intelligence in many of their acts. Some later scientists, whilst holding that instinct is the dominating factor in animals, confound it with "reflex action," "automatism," etc., as stated above. As I find I cannot agree with either view, I propose to examine briefly some of the facts which disclose the nature and functions of the psychological activities on which these theories rest.

I see no reason why animals should not have a power of mind to adjust themselves to their conditions by discursive methods, after the manner of man.

I cannot delay upon any activity within the physique which is reflex in character and, therefore, wholly beyond the mind's power to attemper, such as the circulation of the blood, etc. Physical cravings or appetites, propensities, etc., are common to animal and man, and shall not be enlarged upon.

I may emphasize here, however, as bearing on

what I shall urge later, that the physical activities of diverse organisms are as diverse in character as the organisms in which they act, and that they can make only such appeals as will conform to the diverse intelligences addressed.

Bearing the above statements in mind, it suggests itself that when we come to animals we are mooting questions of comparative physiological appeals addressed to intelligences differing among themselves, and, from man, phylogenetically.

And here, we have a general consensus of opinion that whatever mind animals and the higher insects may have, it must, like man's, rest on some sort of physical basis for its psychological transformations. But man and animal have different physiques, and they differ in type, much after the manner of a bear from an ox, or a bee from an ichthyosaurus. And this brings us, face to face, with those profound and ineffaceable distinctions which prescribe to each species of animals, and in a lesser degree, to each individual, a rôle of activity adapted to the play of its diversely circumscribed powers, mental and physical. For, as the physiques, say, of a fish and a humming-bird, differ so radically, their physical wants cannot be exactly the same, and so cannot make identical appeals to bird and fish alike. Given a peculiar physique, and you will have a peculiar class of appetites and propensities which determine its scale of being, and limit it to the pursuit of such objects, and to such alone, as will minister to its welfare. It cannot enter upon a career at war with its organism.

Now, I take it that mind and brain, in animals, as in man, are co-acting and co-dependent factors; the one delivering such intra-cerebral excitations as the other can deal with cognitively; the latter passing upon the meaning of what is delivered to it. In other words, mind and the organism must be in perfect accord. For, if not, then one or the other, or both, would be inadequate to the task set before it. For example, in order to perfect vision, we must have a perfect visual organ and a competent perceptive power to confer with the objects presented.

At this point, our facts disclose some important distinctions between man and animals which we cannot ignore.

One consists in the latter's apperceptions being limited in range, whilst man's embrace the universe.

Another takes its departure from the fact, now universally admitted, that many of the lower animals and insects evince a capacity for clear and quick perception surpassing that of man, in sundry particulars.

How do we account for this? Nothing easier, say certain leading thinkers, who class them with instincts, or physical impulses, such as hunger, thirst, etc. But surely, no careful thinker can confound the surpassing intelligence of some animals with the blind, physical impulsions of the organism, many, if not most of which, spring from local secretions which separate one class of animals from another, giving each a several nature.

Still another class of thinkers propound the theory of heredity, with a bias for natural selection, etc. Animals inherit aptitudes for special tasks, these men aver. And they adduce the fact that man can acquire great dexterity of mind and muscle, etc., and argue, thence, that animals and insects cannot only acquire singularly clear perceptions and aptitudes, but pass them over to their progeny, who have the fun of using them instinctively, much like little sucklings. Now, I can readily assent to the theory that animals, insects, etc., do *acquire* knowledge, precisely as man does; and if they do, where is the need of explaining their acts by aggrandizing their dumb instincts, seeing that all your dexterity of muscle, etc., was acquired by the intellect and not by instinct? The productive efficiency is the intellect, and so, if we inherit anything, it must come of the ancestor who was productive of the thing inherited. But this whole thing of heredity is badly complicated by the doctrine of reversion to (it may be) some stupid ancestor who might impart a huge momentum of dulness, quite as infallibly as any one who acquired special dexterities of mind or body. For, in a question of this kind, who can tell whether the progeny has been fecundated from the graves of good men or of the bad; from Jupiter Tonans or Juno; from Solon or his mother; from Socrates or Xanthippe! And whose heart has not given place to mingled feelings of aversion and piteous interest, on first coming to a knowledge of the many torn and mutilated fragments of humanity persistently reappearing, generation after generation, in families whose lineage can be traced back through a long line of ancestors ?   However, I agree that animals and man can pass over to their descendants any dexterity or habit acquired, but that is because the ancestor is an experienced *teacher*, and is at pains to impart what he knows to his progeny and familiars.   And a habit thus acquired might well be mistaken for a so-called instinct.

Still another and fatal objection to this theory is that, notwithstanding man has an immeasurable capacity for acquiring dexterity of mind and muscle, yet his posterity, even if he could pack it off to them by heredity, would be in no better condition to equal insects and animals in their special conceptions and clearer cognitions, than the ancestor was himself.   And it seems to me, therefore, that another theory, more in keeping with the facts, may be propounded ; and it may be precisely stated as follows: The astounding facility and clearness of perception displayed by these latter is backed by an intellectual endowment specially qualified for essaying the tasks allotted to them, *but denied to man.*

Their level of capacity has been determined by the same law that determined that of man.   Human intelligence which widens with the universe is not equal to the task of working up the materials which are local to, nor of discriminating and appropriating the food substances of, say, for instance, a fish in the bottom of the ocean.

But the mind of a fish is definitely qualified and

appointed for accomplishing that task. And therefore the reason why the fish can do this, and man cannot, lies in the fact that the former has a physique whose blind cravings can be sated only by an access of mental power, specially fitted to conceive and evalue his piscatorial wants. Whereas, on the other hand, man has no power of mind, so to identify himself with either the physique or mind of a fish as to appreciate the latter's cravings, adopt his habits, and struggle with his environment.

A human intelligence alone can appease a human appetite, an animal only an animal appetite. And if so, why postulate an instinct for either?

It seems plain, then, that because animals and insects have unique organisms, they must also have unique wants, and if so, they must be ministered to by an intelligence uniquely qualified to provide for them.

For their organisms are furnished with the peculiar secretions which provide for and specialize their appetites, cravings, etc.

And therefore, may we say that even the environment, local to different beings, is, for the most part, that which is determined by the unique cast of their minds and physiques. For mind, everywhere, is the dominant factor employed in selecting an environment the materials of which can be remodelled to suit the physique with which it is mated; anything in the teachings of evolutionists to the contrary notwithstanding.

The distinctive tasks appointed to the different classes of beings are determined by a God-given nature which enables them to select and make use of the powers of exterior nature, in the interest cf wants discursively educed.

And if this is so, it results, as necessarily as a consequence from a principle, that the sensations, impulses, etc., of animals must speak to them in a language with many thousand effective inflections utterly unknown to man's wider reach of vision.

On the other hand, why should not animals have a gift of mind competent rapidly to classify and accelerate the perception of such objects as come within reach of their narrower range of vision?

It is to the physiological and psychological nature and conditions of a being, therefore, that we must look, if we would know the active principles which determine what he does. And here I may mention some peculiarities of structure in animals and insects which are designed to meet special needs arising from natures which differ from that of man.

It is now ascertained that the use of compound eyes in some insects "enables them to enjoy distinct vision during rapid flight." Whereas, in the case of a man going at such rapid speed, no distinct impression could be made of objects crossing his visual area. Here, as elsewhere, it is simply a question of comparative psychology and physiology; mind and physique co-acting in the performance of tasks prescribed by the law for their interdependent activities. And yet, within the field of performance allotted to each, it is not more unreasonable for animals to surpass man in celerity and clearness of

N

perception, within their narrower horizon, than for man to surpass them in his world-wide constructive conceptions.

I mention, here, some few concrete examples in support of these views, though the argument embraces all creatures. Consider the bee and its wax, the spider and its thread, and the viscid and other secretions of many other insects, along with the special aptitudes acquired by each of the above. Now, it is readily apprehended that these creatures could not at all act upon a knowledge of these diverse anatomical structures, so furnished, neither could they interpret their offices in respect of the physical and rational needs they shadow forth, if they were not part and parcel of an organism intimately connected with the diverse mental powers appointed to conceive and act upon their dissimilar intimations. And this is the rationale of all that keen, sharp, quick intelligence displayed by some animals and insects. They have a mind specially appointed and qualified for discerning and appreciating the unique animal impulsions, native to their diversely appointed physiques.

XI

And now, at the last moment before I close, I am led to make a further explanation: In remarking upon the resemblances and differences of the human and animal intelligence, I felt constrained to express a high opinion of the latter, holding that, within the pale of its nature and possibilities, an animal could reason as correctly and clearly as man, protesting, nevertheless, that the similarity of their mental powers and sensorial data furnished no evidence that an animal was furnished with a sweep of mental vision, and power of elaboration of data, equal to that of man. On the contrary, I hold that to each is given a power of mind adapted to construct his own world of egoism and personal satisfactions, in precise conformity to his several ability to appreciate the significance of the things which can be made to contribute to his welfare. And this remits the one, as well as the other, to a nature and destiny whose barriers neither can surmount.

Each can reason and act upon reasons, within the confines prescribed by his nature and confronting environment, because to each is appointed a measure of mental power suited to his nature and environment. And therefore, as thus constituted and conditioned, an animal can frame and put to a determinate use a certain kind and number of conceptions that will appease a certain kind and number of wants, peculiar to an animal and denied to man. A definite physique and mind, definitely correlated for a conjoint work, is the measure and promise of all man, or animal, can do; and as thus empowered and restricted, each is left free to seek his individual wants.

As illustrating these views, I recall an incident or two which transpired when we were children, and which may serve to place my contention in clearer outline before the reader. In those halcyon days, we companioned with an intelligent cur that had discovered a habit of running *away from* the hares in a direct line to their holes in the ground, and from that position running them down at his pleasure. As a matter of course, in the dawn of childhood, we, his companions, were more than delighted with such wonderful feats. But we were destined to see more of the surprising and surpassing power of mind in our poor dumb favorite.

For, once upon a time, he kept up a prolonged and deep-mouthed barking the major part of a summer's day, away down in the bottom lands, about a mile from our house. The evening twilight was approaching, when a half-dozen of us little children, our hearts flushed with rosiest anticipations, toddled down to where he still kept up his fierce barking. To us, in our infantile innocence and inexperience, it was an outing of eager interest and wonderment, which the rude touch of time, and a wider experience, had not yet robbed of its awful significance. The dog had unearthed a den of foxes, nestled at the end of a hole excavated far within the soft ground, and was busy destroying the whelps, — a feat which he accomplished soon after our arrival there! And so it happened that, just at this time, the old mother fox hove in sight of this scene of slaughter, and the dog espying her, we were made spectators to the philosophy of a race for life or death.

I need not say that we were wildly excited. The fox made for a precipitous cliff on the bank of the little river along which she ran, and about a mile from where we stood. The dog, for his part, was

familiar with the approaches to the cliff, and its
crumpled folds and fissures, — the safe refuge for
all the foxes for miles around.   I should have said
that the river here describes a complete semicircle
between where we were standing and the aforementioned cliff.   As I said, the fox ran along the
river, and, of course, with the semicircle, so that, in
case she were hotly pursued, she could take advantage of the undergrowth that fringed its border.
So much for the fox.   And now, you may imagine
the amazement of, at least, one of the little children
when he saw that his aforetime sagacious cur would
not run *after the fox at all*, indeed, would not so
much as deign to look at her, but kept heading forward along an inner line pointing *directly* to the
cliff, and four or five hundred yards off to one side
of the fox.   Off to one side of, and not looking
toward her!   And we poor, little innocents were
sore confounded and mystified for many a weary
day — for, to us, it seemed passing strange that our
once conspicuously intelligent dog should now run
so witlessly off to one side of the fox!   But then, as
we afterward learned, the dog made his point and
captured the fox; and this reassured us somewhat.

And now, after the lapse of more than sixty
years, it seems abundantly plain that both dog and
fox alike had been doing some remarkably clear
thinking, evincing consummate judgment, and practical insight in mastering the details of a problem
involving the issues of life and death.   And in all
this, they were the equals of any man.   The dog,
in particular, must have reasoned from his mul-

tiform experiences of the behavior of hares and foxes to the particular case of the fox and the foot race. But he could not have done this without resorting to some process of rational elaboration which would call for the exercise of the resources of comparison, discriminating judgment, and inference from facts, — solving thus the difficult problems which grow out of a present and pressing emergency by a grand *induction* from former experiences to the case in hand. It is to be understood, however, that this range of mental vision and elaboration found in animals never extends much beyond these and similar experiences. For both dog and fox equally are at touch with a physical and mental nature which restricts them to conceptions framed in conformity to their definitely appointed animal possibilities, and to nothing beyond.

For instance, to compare them with the toddling infants who witnessed their race in the field, neither of them could conceive, much less build, a house in the sand, with, say, chimneys, doors, rooms, windows, etc., not to mention sundry other, little toilette appointments, constructed of chips and sticks, cobs, sods, rocks, mosses, and what not — such as the just mentioned children, heirs to larger conceptive visions, not seldom conceive and build, and, mayhap, on that very day did conceive and build. For, the inferences and deductions upon which a human being acts, though, as a matter of course, limited by his human nature, embrace the bolder flights of constructive vision which inform and empower a human soul.

We conclude, therefore, that the nature of any creature determines the character, and limits the scope, of his intellections, even the individual point of view he will take when attacking the problems of life and personal well-being.

But, if you want to put all thought of a correct psychology to grief, only keep up this dusky prattle about animals, and even man, acting on "instinct," "reflex action," etc., so much affected, nowadays, by some leading scientists. An animal, for example, simply takes an animal view of himself and surroundings, and he is just as competent to reason from his nature and surroundings to his peculiar needs as man, from his nature and surroundings, to his peculiar needs. Let us have man or animal to discover all he can discover of the significance of things, inner and outer, and connect all he can discover of them with the personal, individual, and social requirements indicated by his nature and surroundings.

CHAPTER XVII

THOUGHT AND EXTERIOR POWERS CONTRASTED

THINGS exterior do impress mind, but is the latter on that account only receptive of the impression, only subjective in their presence? Might not thought, for its part, be as active, aggressive, and discrete in its own way and by virtue of its own resources as any exterior power?

I

Observe that the appeal is to mind, and not to anything exterior, for an opinion. And if this is so, it seems clear that the former is already in court with an antecedent claim that everything in the universe is bound to respect. For, as Hamilton expresses it: If we know everything through mind, we must know mind beyond doubt, for the paramount reason that we know all else through it.

Now, if thought is thus admittedly such a prepotent affirmative energy, I might retort on the extreme school of sensationists, by disallowing the claims of sensations altogether. For, look at the argument! All I know of mind is a subjectivity seen in my thought and inferences. So, too, all I know of external nature is this same subjectivity, seen as above. Moreover, though I

184

am a unit of body and mind, all I know, and can
know, of either is the same subjectivity, seen also
as above. Am I therefore an idealist? By no
means! I am no more an idealist than a materi-
alist. Thought gives me *both*, and the one is as
solidly and defiantly accredited as the other.
Still, if either has place in thought as a something
affirmed and accredited, it is there on the sole
testimony of the cognitive energy which decisively
avouches a knowledge of it.

Admitting then the presence and power of sensations as unquestionable, what I would contend for
is that mind is not a mere receptive blank, capable
of only witnessing for what is delivered to it by
means of sensorial impressions. It has rational
potencies for achieving knowledges, with which,
in an act of cognition, every exterior potency
has to be brought into sympathetic and helpful
coöperation.

It speaks the word of authority without which
the very being and possibilities of a sensation could
never be called forth. It is a cognitive power, and
so much so that it cannot even receive a sensorial
impression without affirming it by an act of perception or conception. It has a boundless curiosity,
to begin with, and its very life depends on what it
can discover of, and do with, the things of self
and not self. It lives on the power of the ideas
it acquires. And this capacity for thought and
deed, this intellectual power and performance, is so
intrepid that we can scarcely imagine a momen-
tary interval in which we have nothing to do,

without our having, in the selfsame instant, a multitude of things to be done staring us in the face and calling for attention; the intelligence is so promptly and punctually active and aggressive.

Indeed, we cannot take the most indifferent and cursory glance at anything without immediately framing some opinion of its value, as a discovery conceived to be related, in some way, to our interests. And, in all such cases, we advance as we perceive and conceive. Observe a child taking an interest in its childish affairs. Its every thought is in the direction of its welfare, as an individual power diverse from all others, say, to feel its muscular powers; to put some first, faint estimate on the kind attentions of a mother, nurse, etc., to recognize her presence as the frequent source of its happiness, — it may be, as a great outside *person*, or *alter ego*, caring for its whims, wants, or hurts. And here, beyond doubt, we have a personal power, at one and the same moment affirming and contrasting itself with things and potencies not itself.

Thought, then, is a distinct entity which founds on its discursive resources for acquiring power and action of its own. But if sensations give it ideas, then we have informations without the rational scrutiny needed to fetch them. We have not found truth, but it has found us. And if this is so, it is imposed on us, and we are not free.

However, let us examine this point carefully. We hold to the fundamental postulate that nothing is known except through the active intervention of mind. From earliest infancy onward, this our thinking equipment has to discover and affirm every fact for our guidance, noting intently the very first coming of sensations, and so entering upon a broader plane of exploration and discovery. The mind takes cognitive interest in these sensorial impressions, and straightway proceeds to form a more intimate acquaintance with entities and activities exterior to itself, acquiring power to act in accordance with what it affirms of them and their mission.

Indeed, it is incumbent on us to know things not ourselves; affirming and appreciating their content of attributes, actions, and relations, lest otherwise we be at their mercy. It is to be observed that we are not claiming for thought the position of an isolated or independent entity. It is surrounded with a universe of other entities which it essays to know, and must know as entities coupled in some way with its welfare; must commune with these as things of meaning, each having a special significance imparted to it by Him who gave them place to sport their powers hereabouts, and must make all it can learn of them so entirely its own that it can employ what it learns of them, as a personal power promotive of its own good.

It is to be remarked that I make due allowance for the extra-mental potencies which act on, or with, our thought, endeavoring to point out their relation to the volitional and personal factors which call out our educated, or personal, traits and wants. For the reader should now understand that, whenever we have the rational impulsions called *desires*, they act as our personal motors or powers and so act because called forth by the rational and constructive appreciations that beget personal considerations and a personal outlook.

II

Knowledge is not made over to us by any power different from an ordinary discursion. We have to acquire it as best we can. We have to discover our rational humanities, and so be moved to act from rational considerations and trained impulsions. There is a close brotherhood of mental and physical forces in man. They are roofed together from childhood, and constitute an original, or autochthonous, brood co-acting in furtherance of a conjoint work. Some contribute to the animal economy, such as sensations, physical cravings, appetites, etc. But all these blind physical factors occupy sheltered retreats, speechless and sightless, until they are made to disclose their mission by the party that intermeddles with wisdom.

Quite on the confines of this close brotherhood is that vast horde of physical and material entities — our outdoor neighbors — who people the immensities of time and space with the mind of God. It were well that these physical, vital, and remoter parties should make a call upon the thoughtful party. And they are now, face to face, in actual contact, and exchanging civilities.

Now, what is the effect of this exterior visitation? Simply a notification of business of importance to both parties, the exterior parties proclaiming in effect: "Try and forget it. We have our rude way of coming into your presence. Do not be the least disturbed. No harm meant. We are commissioned to furnish you with a specimen of our peculiar dynamics. Here are some sensorial impressions to your hand in the sensorium for your thoughtful appreciation. We are but pursuing the letter of the enabling act which prescribes and limits our functions,— even as it does yours. And we are doing our part to promote the social intercourse, if not welfare, of both. We cannot act anti-socially, even if we would. It is neither our fault nor yours, if this our social compact and intercourse should entail some grave responsibilities and rough experiences upon our intelligent brother. Sufficient for all that is the Omniscient. We have fulfilled our mission. We trust we have not been offensively intrusive. Business is business. Still, may we not look for you to give us, in turn, a touch of your friendly regards? We leave you to your reflections. Good morning to you!"

III

The order of treatment of such a vast subject leads me to speak of another aspect of our problem. I am referring to efforts made to confound the contents of our sensations with thought, feeling (emotion), and volition, etc. For we are informed that these latter are simply complexes of sensations, that is to say, of elements, each essentially similar to blue, hot, cold, sour, etc. This we deny *in toto.*

I had thought that I had said enough to give thought and sensations their proper places in the scheme of interaction devised for the diverse factors concerned. But here is perhaps the proper place to define more precisely this very matter of the power and interdependence of the two.

Every sensation, so this doctrine runs, has a quality and intensity which represent the nature and strength of the stimulus which determines the thought, emotion, etc., of the thinker. And this, we are told, is a deliverance of science, which is incontrovertible and final. But how much truer to science, and sensations as well, it would be, if, whilst allowing for all a sensation can do, science would allow for all thought can do?

I am under constraint to my practicable limits, proposing to place before my reader only a few of the controlling facts quietly ignored by the scientist.

I grant the power, stress, and tone of sensations. Thought does not propose to interfere, indeed has no need to interfere, with the nature and powers of things, external or internal. What I contend for is that this can never explain a state of mind which has an appointed outfit of resources of its own, for dealing with sensations and their tone. Finite thought and sensation must hang together, as contrasted but co-active factors, let the stress and tone of either be what they may. But that any normal peculiarity of sensation should antagonize the distinctive efficiencies of thought, or that of thought, those of sensation, is to the last degree unpsychological and false.   I have, all along, contended that sensation has power, and quality of power, sufficient to impress thought with its peculiar dynamics, arresting its attention, and so opening a way for the assertion of its cognitive transformations.   And this is but a pre-arrangement of the Creator for establishing and conserving the interaction and co-action of the diverse factors concerned.

But, says an objector, what becomes of the tone and temper, dominant stress, etc., of a sensation? Well, I shall now attend to that point too.   And I would propose to my objectors simply to let both thought and sensation have a tone and temper of their own, undisturbed and undisputed, and so preserve both, intact.   Let the sensorial efficiencies deliver an impression in the sensorium, and let thought do its own thinking, and the tone and temper of both will be preserved.   I am intently regarding the sensation and its tone as seen in the sensorium and nowhere else, and inquiring how that tone is there set up and what sets it up.

And I affirm that the tone and stress of sensation is as much set up genetically by mind as by the exterior potency.   It takes *both* to set them up. For whatever they may be in anything placed outside of the mind's coöperative efficiencies, the tone and stress found in a sensation (and that is the only evidence we have for them) depend as much on mind for being and action as upon the sensorial impression made in the brain.   And if they step forth as distinguishable elements of a sensation, they will have to undergo some careful manipulation at the hands of thought.

I deny to mind the least power to fledge exterior things with either tone or pressure proper to their nature. And I am as emphatic in denying to these latter the least power to fledge mind with any tone or pressure proper to its several nature. The inhibition applies to both. But conceding the tone and pressure of things exterior to be what it may, mind can lay claim to the diverse, but correlative, power of reacting upon that tone and pressure with a cognitive tone and pressure peculiar to itself, and estranged from any external power. It has a life and growth of its own furnished with intellectual peculiarities of its own, and goes out to try conclusions with exterior impressions, and so make conquest of their mode and manner of being, gathering power and building up its counter-activities, as it captures idea after idea from the static and dynamic naturalism of things exterior. For, with every idea captured, is born a personal, that is to say, an emotional or desiderative vehemence, which is consummated in conduct or acts held in conscious contrast with exterior powers and transformations. For we are now in the power of our thoughts, and can make our points as we think.

Part IV

PERSONAL AND VOLUNTARY POWER OF INFORMATIONS

CHAPTER XVIII

DESIRES AND EMOTIONS

IN other connections I have maintained the thesis that knowledge is ours by right of discovery, and that, being ours, its power is also ours, for our guidance and governance. The same view obtains in the treatment of desires and emotions. For these are nothing but the stress of our informations manifested as *personal* or voluntary power in the realm of conduct. And this view is the keystone in the arch of free determinations.

I

Let us carefully consider the problem. We transport us to the time, when we are inspired by the aims and purposes that express our desires and emotions. At this period, we are permitted to think that we have measurably completed the discoveries and distinctions which inform and educe our rational wants.

And, here, it is important to remark that the birth of our rational wants is the birth of personal or voluntary powers. This seems evident. But, for the moment, let us inquire what is the fortune and function of the desires and emotions which we may not now embrace? For we see them tempora-

rily replaced by others which emphasize our present or prevailing views.   And yet they continue
along with us, as psychological possessions, reappearing, it may be, on a sudden, as a provisional
instigation to conduct, and though we may repulse
their demands, we cannot repress their importunities.

If this be so, then we may be prompted to act
from two sets of desires, one active, the other
potential.   The former may be likened to a man-
of-war steering in the face of the gales.   The latter
is more like a league of gunboats attached to the
command, and subject to the orders, of the admiral.

What, then, is the office of these floating desires?
We have seen that our native appetencies possess
the trait of an original orientation for *mind*.   But
our floating desires possess that of an acquired
orientation for *conduct*.   For they are trained, and,
therefore, personal motors, and show the influence
of a careful teacher.

But if trained, then they are not to be classed
with native potencies.   And yet, as their orientation was determined by some *prior* thought, their
impulsion must set in before a present one, after
the manner of a native appetency.   Nevertheless,
as their intimations are traceable solely to some
foregoing thought, they are to be regarded as our
own, *i.e.*, personal and voluntary impulsions.   And
so, when they emerge as a present spur to conduct,
they occupy the border ground which shades off
into both past and present.

They can, therefore, make a strong personal

appeal to the authority of reason. If, however, on due consideration, they should antagonize our present views, we may dismiss their appeal. Still, they are a fairly correct and forcible demarkation for conduct, exhibiting a diversity of character and vehemence whose every feature reveals some trace of previous thought.

II

Reverting now to a former illustration, I may remark that man's position, touching these aforetime trained impulsions, or floating desires, is not exactly that of the shepherd to the fold, seeing that they were called forth by his voluntary procurement, and that he controls them as his own voluntary efficiencies. Hence, their power over conduct is not a question between him and another something, but between him and his own something. Stated otherwise, it is not between him and what is not his, but between him and what is his.

III

I turn now to the subject of active desires mediated in the present. I explain by remarking that we have an original capacity for acquiring such desires and emotions as depend on the ability to discover their satisfying objects. For every rational satisfaction is an object of desire solely through the mind's power of conception and elaboration. Knowing an object, once for all, we must also know why we should desire it; our intelligence ever going before, to witness for our desires.

Indeed, if any sane mind, turned twenty, can entertain rudimental impulses unchallenged of thought, it is because nothing of superior dignity can impress it.

One securely rational imports his own desires from his own substance (here actively thoughtful and voluntary), and puts his own substance (explained as above) into whatever affects conduct, be it regarded as information, emotion, desire, or what not.

And, therefore, I affirm that our freedom is won by a carefully intelligent sifting and testing in manifold ways of that which we conceive will contribute something desirable, or otherwise undesirable, enabling us to choose the one, and discard the other. For the conceit of mind is everywhere trying conclusions in respect of what we should desire, and we put our best thought into what we are pondering, and incline to it, or not, by an act of judgment affirming choice or ultimate desire.

Reflect a moment. Make me altogether human, but endowed with the brutish proclivities of a beast: How could I perceive, much less prize and prefer, the qualities of human excellence, to be desiring them? We must have a human soul and its broader sweep of vision: That is to say, we must have the power of human ideas or informations, to give us the psychological competency for appreciating what can placate or repel a human being; for we must act upon informations which shut us up to final choice as completed desire.

Every fact of experience attests this.   Here is a

class of emotions which spring from the contemplation of objects of beauty, or else the sublime and wonderful. In the presence of such objects, who is not either thrilled with ecstasy, or subdued into awe? But why? It is all in the quality and qualifications of mind. A dog would speed by the pyramids of Egypt, as heedless of their majestic significance as of the sorriest protoplasmic dust beneath his feet. He hies on, outspeeding the award of even a passing glance. But then, he has no mind for either protoplasmic or pyramidal grandeurs. That is all! Intellectual, or moral, or æsthetic sense in an empty pate is a nonentity that can by no means be baited into being.

But man's mental competency is ceaselessly gendering the emotions and desires which crown him lord of the humanities. We must *appreciate* the æsthetic significance of such objects, ere we are permitted to feel the characteristic emotions. And, in order to this, we shall have to cultivate a class of refined conceptions whose presence alone can inspire the appropriate emotions and desires.

It will behoove us, therefore, to see our way out to the objects specially appointed to inspire us with such desires and emotions as our human intelligence can elicit and sanction, imparting to them the life-giving force of our conceptions. For they can never become factors for conduct, save as they are inspired by and walk with our thought.

Emotions and desires must have power, but then, they must energize as we think, carrying out in all literalness the force of our thoughts, as I wish to make evident, later on. Even now as I write, I can almost visualize some object divinely fair and bright. Suppose though that this reconstructive power of the imagination is lost to me. How could I, then, have either emotion or desire for the object? It seems plain, therefore, that some mental or moral power must be resorted to, in order to my having a reason for my interest in the object desired.

It is absolutely impossible for any human mind to desire at the bidding of a *blind* impulse. In the strictest psychological sense, therefore, the self determines conduct by making choice, or effectuating some final desire; the choice or final desire simply expressing, or emphasizing, our personal preference or prevailing reason or opinion. Desire is a reason personally attempered. *We desire only as we think.*

IV

One may contend, however, that as many of our desires are implicated with our native cravings and propensities, they prompt, and in prompting affect, conduct, in spite of the power of thought. This misconception has been freshly gone upon in former pages, but as it turns up here, we may remark upon it in passing.

I have explained the function of thought as the genetic source of emotions and desires in contrast with all these involuntary forces, and shall not therefore go into all that problem here.

But I may be allowed to remark, further, that if one should not become deeply moved, or else supported by some form of emotion or desire when contemplating the curious and persistent strivings of his blind, animal impulses, he could never take an interest in their study sufficient to put him on the track of their rational explanation. As it is, he remarks and ponders their significance, and so is moved to discover all knowledge which will prepare him for leading them forth in the ways of thought.

The truth is, as heretofore explained, we start with a stock of native propensities which, as native, are sheerly animal and blind impulsions, emerging outside of thought, as irrational and involuntary instigations providing for its advent. And they have no other function. And here I beg to repeat that that which is in a state of natural priority to what we can intelligently desire is in no position to take in hand the peculiar tasks of thought,— these being subsequent, cognitive, and, therefore, personal achievements of the awakened intelligence. For thought must have command of its own resources, ere it can have a reason for acting, springing from a view of what it can personally desire or prefer. And when it has command of these, it moves on a plane of personal responsibility for its every desire. And thenceforth, it will have its own desire, in its own way of thinking, or none at all. Otherwise, it would lack power to mediate its own impulsions, and couple them with aims and objects rationally affirmed and sanctioned.

But granting, now, that these blind impulses do blindly prompt to action, let me ask, How can that antagonize thought in the slightest degree? The fact is indisputable that there can never be any prompting by any impulse independent of our seeing something in an object which prompts the desire, or moves us to desire it. And mind alone can do that.

Now, who or what does this seeing or thinking; who affirms the object desired, if not the responsible actor, man? So then, if this be so, the real prompting is done by a desire mediated by the power of thought. For all desire comes of, and is born with, some thought, and so is really but an expression of its personal force or power.

It is evident, therefore, that a mere blind impulse fails to account for man's acts. He is not quite rawer than the rawest specimen of an animal. He reasons and acts with his reasons, as indeed he *acts them*, whenever he makes choice or fulfils desire, for fulfilling a desire is, and can be, nothing but actualizing choice or preference, ultimating the personal power of some thought.

From all which, it is evident that the elaborating and constructive efficiencies of mind give us voluntary, not necessary, actions; intelligent desires, not blind promptings; even ultimate desires, and personal power and responsibility. And the general conclusion reached is that whatever man does is done in accordance with his rational convictions, and that, whenever he acts from reason, he may have both desires and their objective satisfactions, as he reasons, and because of his reasons.

And this means, further, that we may put a term

to any floating desires that we might go upon in the unguarded moments of sinful solicitations. For we are free, moral agents only when we can make some choice final, in the light of a judicious view of our personal responsibility. I may therefore lay down the two following propositions as incontrovertible : —

1. Man discovers what to choose or desire, training his mind to a knowledge and appreciation of such objects, and such satisfactions, as he can prefer, or choose, or desire; employing thus the energy found in some intelligent appreciation of the object desired; that is to say, desire must lean upon thought, — here opinion or information of some kind, — in order that it may be responsible as *choice*.

2. Man must know what to choose, as a responsible *person* walking in the light of educated or voluntary impulsions; and so he walks by the power of the thoughts which beget the desires for which he is responsible.

The following illustration may serve to support my contention. I am beholding a rainbow with emotions of wildering pleasure. Whence come all these fervid emotions? They are unquestionably mine, if not by former experience and personal espousal, at least by present, intelligent, propæ-deutic elaboration. The assertion may seem bold, but they cannot be rightly described as prompting me at all, — they are so intimately my own. Every effort of thought, past or present, has contributed its quota of personal power to give me the joy of

such a resplendent display of prismatic colors.
And now that I am possessed of the corresponding
emotions, it is not impertinent to repeat that it
would not be strictly correct to say: It is a question
between me and my emotions. Nay, rather, it is
I myself, with the susceptibilities I have fostered,
taking pleasure in an object brought before my
thought, to the extent of my capacity for affirming
such elements of the beautiful stored in nature.
For the gospel of such a glad revelation of nature
can never be enjoyed in the absence of mind to
appreciate the revelation.

Now will any one dare say that these and kindred emotions, or desires, are the promptings of
that which acts without the intervention of my
intelligence and vivid appreciations? Have not
the desires which prompt me been made mine by a
whole life of achievement in the domain of mind,
morals, and æsthetics? I am moved toward what
I desire by a power of thought and its careful distinctions, and I enter upon choice or ultimate desire
with the eyes of my judgment opened upon the
object, and I enter upon what I do by projecting
this very thought into the thing to be done.

Yes, pleasing were those emotions of the beautiful, and taught of all the humanities of thought to
rejoice in its ways and do them.

V

I am still debating the ability of a responsible
creature to conceive reasons which move him to act.

Let me vary the mode of inquiry somewhat. The

finger responds with but little previous training to the stimulus of thought. On the other hand, the moral factor has to be sedulously and continually trained to act with foresight of consequences, ere it can entertain, much less finally act upon, its peculiar *stimuli.*

The office of the finger is denoted by its obvious structure, and so the analogy between it and the moral factor might seem to be imperfect. But if we could teach the finger to discharge some nobler function determined by the exigencies of a higher life to be entered upon when properly instructed, such as that of intellectual power and personal responsibility, we might bring home to our conception an instance of intense and vivid training parallel to that of our own voluntary experience. Now it is just here, and in this connection, that I am led to observe that the desire centre, *when trained,* responds as promptly to the authority of reason as does the finger. The power of thought begets a desire as promptly as it can release and control the blind forces shut up in the finger.

Permit me to explain further. Let us imagine that we are now in possession of much that reason affirms to be desirable; objects for which we may strive. For we have affirmed their points of attraction and struggle for their possession. Now, all this is in the line of our voluntary powers, or personal and responsible achievements. And, therefore, it has not been our fortune, so far, to detect any element of necessity in any promptings of the emotions or desires involved.

But after all, do they not often make a very urgent appeal to reason? Yes, very often. And so here may be our chance to trump up necessity. I call for the appeal. A presbyterial overture goes before the synod. The overturists either suggest some action, or ask for instructions. The synod may, *if it chooses*, act with the suggestion, or it may lay down a rule of conduct for the inferior court. As it is a petition for advice or a rule of action, it acts finally, and that settles the case for the overturists.

Now suppose we take the appeals of our floating desires to be distinctly separable from any power of thought or morals to give them their wonted efficiency — though this supposition is contrary to fact! Even then, the fact of their making an appeal to reason is a confession of subordination. And now, when they obey the latter's behests, they stand in an attitude analogous to one of our physical members moving at the command of thought.

But now, let us suppose that we have long since made the desires we have on hand to be *our own*, and this, whether our success in their elicitation and cultivation could be commended or not. What would, then, be the character of their appeals? Evidently, *our own*, be they good or bad. But, if our own, and elicited by our own efforts, where would be the taint of necessity?

Any impulsion thus made our own (and for any reason) is, and can be, nothing but a personal and voluntary vehemence which bespeaks our thought, coming into being and taking orders, as it does, from the power that mediates every possible emotion or desire — even what should and what should not, be desired. For the good or bad of what is ours has been pondered and felt from aforetime in the forum of reason, and we have to act on any, the last instigation, proceeding from the last phase of our desires, as we did on any previous one; we choose or reject it at our peril.

And I contend that this dependence of all our emotional or desiderative impulsions is so all-embracing and thoroughgoing that, at any time we would do something, there is not one single emotion or desire which is not conditioned by some power of mind, for any force it may have, when rising into consciousness. For here is concentrated all the antecedent experiences of the soul, embracing the unbroken continuity of the whole series, such as every new thought and its power, even emotions and desires keeping step with the thoughts that inspired them.

So much for the power of thought and its inseparable train of emotions and desires.

VI

It seems plain, therefore, that neither appetencies, nor floating desires, nor for that matter any force, exterior or not, can trench upon the prerogatives of thought, choice, or voluntary determination. They are all bound by the enabling clause of the fundamental law which prescribes and limits their functions, just as the man, as a whole, is similarly limited and bound.

He, too, has to submit to a law for his finite powers. He cannot alter the nature of any of his members, say again, a finger. He can, indeed, command a power which will move it. And, if it move, it is because, say, of his desire to move it. The bones, muscles, and jointed, prehensile structure, etc., are furnished by Another, and he, for his part, can neither annihilate these furnished materials, nor vacate their functions. But he can (and that is all I claim) summon into being every idea, emotion, or desire needed for such movements of the finger, or other physical members, as will actualize the (now) personal and voluntary power involved in moving it, or else required for any of the tasks of life set before him.

CHAPTER XIX

CHOICE AND MORAL SANCTIONS

THE problem in this chapter is to determine the function of those ultimating informations which cover acts of choice and personal responsibility. I recall some distinctions. Our reasons, viewed as intellections, express intellectual power, but viewed as emotions or desires they express personal power; and both are employed in acts of choice and morals. This will be further explained, later on.

I

To begin with a case of moral lapse or declension. Not seldom do we choose to indulge a literal demand of some sinful desire or purpose, or motive, moral protests to the contrary notwithstanding. Then, on the other hand, we may assert the claims of our better humanity in opposition to the former. This looks embarrassing; for at first glance, one would think that the force of a rational and moral conviction would always be with the right, and that, therefore, our personal preference would always be with the right. But this would be a grave mistake. Sufficient allowance must be made for our frail humanities, especially for the daring and perilous sweep of conception, in dealing with questions of practical conduct, under conditions of temptation, alternative choice, and personal responsibility.

We have choice between good and bad, but we must reap the inevitable consequences of our choice. And though we make a bad choice, we can never question the authority and blessedness of morals, albeit even morals are conditioned on a law which protests the divine right of choice and its tremendous responsibilities.

Again, the idea or conception of right and wrong, as also that of choice between them, are equally achievements of mind. But mind cannot employ these conceptions at their best, unless they are maintained in their integrity.

Furthermore, the sanctity of morals can neither be weakened nor effaced, except as the right of choice between right and wrong is effaced or weakened, through its sinful abuse. This will be explained more fully as we proceed.

Ponder another distinction. The mere discovery of the idea of right and wrong, or even that of choice between them, can never destroy the right of choice. We shall have to look otherwhere for that fearful undoing which overwhelms the right of choice.

It would certainly be a surprising discovery, if on a discovery of a moral find, the discoverer should discover that he had thereby lost the right of responsible choice. The moment such a discovery would be made, that very instant the obligatory force of morals would cease. Displace the right of choice, and even the conception of morals will cease with it, as will be explained in the sequel.

Lost it may be, however, — but far otherwise. Only let one *choose sin* HABITUALLY, and he will know of the process; because he will have so fostered his evil propensities that they will *compel* the promptest subserviency to their behests.

It would appear, then, that there is nothing in moral conceptions inimical to the right of choice. The obligation, though divine and because divine, is not *compulsory*. It appeals to us through the force of righteous convictions, imploring us to behold the way of life, and ponder the mischiefs of a wrong choice, and with it a profligate violation of our conception of right.

Now, in all this matter of an appeal to our loftier humanities, we fail to see anything like the annihilation of the right of choice. On the contrary, it is an earnest, loving, tearful, and solemn appeal to our discretion, remitting the final decision to the tribunal of judgment and personal responsibility. And, as thus viewed, it becomes a problem for careful thought, a matter for conscience and information, — a search for ideas which are valued and employed in the affairs of personal conduct, like other informations, at our peril.

We may well pause, in view of the fearful retributions which follow the wanton disregard of such an appeal. But here is a temptation to indulge some sinful inclination, very persuasive to certain latitudinarian proclivities of choice. We contrast this with the life-giving principles of rectitude. The alternatives are good or bad, right or wrong. We have choice among the reasons *pro* and *con.*   What happens ?   The sinful reasons prevail !

We choose sin, and take the consequence !

II

Now it so happens that I hear an indignant reader exclaiming: "You have opened to us a view of the divine authority of right, and yet you say : 'We can prefer sin.'   What then becomes of the divinity of the obligation of morals ?   What is clothed with divine sanctions should forever be the strongest reason, and so prevail against one not so clothed.   And do you not concede that the strongest reason always prevails ?"

My reader seems to be clever, but a trifle touchy.

However, facts are implacable.   We can, and do sin.   Indeed, we are moral agents solely through this stubborn power of choice between good and bad.   Yes, we are so human, and so taught of our frail humanities, that we can take delight in naughty preferences and sinful pleasures.   But if so, we must have reasons for it, for one cannot sin without them.   And, therefore, are we determined to sin by them.   And if thus determined, they must be to us (gifted as we are with the power to choose between diverse, and even opposite, ways of life) the most urgent reasons.   For it is quite impossible for us to act on any reason which is overborne by stronger ones.

You may be dazed by an order of things that permits sin.   But there is a wisdom above man's.   The truth is as I have stated it.   We cannot be moral agents without this power to choose between good and bad, — at our peril. And, beyond doubt, we have a varied experience of both, and must have inclined to sin, for some reason, acting with it, or not, as we had power to overcome, or else resist, the evil. The power of our moral convictions, if not wholly blotted out, will assist us in the struggle. But repeated and profligate indulgence will, in time, become the dominant factor.

I am arguing from the force of the reasons present to the sinner, in an act of choice.

Mark the nature of his soul.

His reasons may be good or bad in the forum of conscience, — an authority he never questions, so long as he can appreciate the normal significance of the two. For what is sin but a violation of right whilst acknowledging its sanctity? But now that he has dallied with the baser choice, too often and too long, he puts the question evasively before the court of conscience. He feels his obligations and would not part from them. Still, his temper is a little uncertain. He is but awaiting " a more convenient season."

He continues speciously. " I grant you the magnetic impressiveness of morals, and do it homage, notwithstanding my many lamentable aberrations. But then, it is quite in keeping with my views of choice and personal responsibility for me to have an adequate, *practical* standard of comparison between right and wrong ; and I can have none until I have had a sharpened experience of the two, easy to hand, for any trustworthy estimate of their rival claims. And, even though I do commit sin, do I not hold me fearfully responsible for my venture?" I am not inclined to endorse this euphemistic, if not fantastic, subterfuge, though, perhaps, the sinner may be assigning *his* reason for the commission, in the hour of temptation and choice. His excuse is no justification. Of this, later on.

And yet it is too true, that when he tramples on the right, with his eyes still open to its sanctity, some sinful reason carries the power that precipitates choice; and with choice of sin, its wasting train of consequences. But, after allowing for all the mischief he does to himself, and that is often irreparable, he may still count upon what is left of his right of choice, as an important aid to discipline and reformation.

The conclusion is irresistible, therefore, that the right of choice is a pervading and constant feature which the mere authority of morals has no power to displace, for, although it can never be asserted independent of moral conceptions, it may not always be upright. Moreover, though one be convinced that, if he give way to the bad, he will wrong his moral compunctions, yet if he does give way, he may still be regarded as maintaining his right of choice, albeit under a sense of moral degradation which, if not relieved, and the right of choice be yet further abused, may ultimately disable the power to choose.

III

But, I am not done with the more serious aspects of the problem. It is to be understood that, though everything must give way to that final phase of information which determines choice and personal responsibility, yet the sinner, meantime, is undergoing a moral declension which is undermining the authority of his moral conceptions. The prerogative of choice, as a normal and beneficent power for good, is being gradually and insidiously blotted out, by as much as sinful practices have sapped the foundations of morals. Moral convictions are losing their wonted force, and the sinner lapses into forbidden paths.

For, if one would preserve intact the right of choice, and, at the same time, be perfectly free, he should choose the right and maintain it firmly through life. He will then learn of a perfect law for both right and choice, good and liberty, which shall bless him in all he does; a law which will uphold the equal primacy of both, so long as he does right.

I make no distinction between the power and right of choice. For our *power* to choose depends on whether we are, and to what extent, free from the despotism of profligate desires, and this involves the right to choose. For if we are slaves to the madness of passions, we shall do their bidding, and so doing, we shall trample under foot both the power and right of choice.

I have explained that the constraint of morals can have no force and no place in conduct, except as mind uncovers the ideas of right and wrong, in order to a choice between them. And I could not imagine a stultification so vacuous as the contention that the mere discovery of such ideas as right and wrong should have the torsionary effect of wresting the right of choice from its foundations. This it cannot do, and is never done, so long as the discoverer is free to put the force of moral convictions into what he does. But if he sin, and particularly, if he persist in it, his very convictions themselves become so utterly debauched that he is no longer able to resist the tyranny of his passions, and so, to that extent, abridges, or loses, the right of choice.

This is not to say that the force of moral conceptions is not a supreme authority to as many as defer to it, by a godly walk and conversation, only that, in the sinner's lapsed condition, the sinner's sinful reasons are the strongest *to him*, — some of his fairer gifts of moral appreciation having undergone a partial deformation. For the power of a moral conception is not the same to the pure and impure. And, to prevent misconception, let me here state explicitly that, if we stoop too often to pick up sin, the day will surely come when we shall dump our shaky, moral compunctions in the mire, and their aforetime office of reformation and righteous repression will forever cease.

And now, to sum up what I have said, I reaffirm that the right of choice is never evicted, so long as we are in a condition to assert it, in opposition to vile practices. But then, on the other hand, I claim that the moral law *is* competent, at all times, to protect this right, if peradventure we have not, meantime, sunk our distinctive humanities beneath its reach, by a reckless abuse of the right of choice.

IV

I am now thinking of some further details which may be needed to support my contention, — confining attention, more particularly, to some of the psychological evidences involved.

Let us say that we have just conceived the idea of right and wrong, as also that of their antithesis, two very important informations, to begin with. For, here we have our first revelation of the essential elements, upon which we found conduct, and the practical honesties and dishonesties of years of responsibility.

A step further leads us to conceive the idea of *choice* between the alternatives, adjudging this choice to be so inseverable from us that we cannot part company from it, and be ourselves, at least so long as it is not literally overborne by the lusts of the flesh, — another important information.

We now take some steps to appraise the value of right or rectitude; and if we come to the conclusion that there is something in it so august that, if we do not give it precedence in comparison with other ideas, we must atone for the incivility in some way, we shall, then, be in a position to make a judicious choice between the alternatives of good and bad, — still another important information.

Here I have brought out the two principles employed in the government of conduct: the right of choice, and the authority of morals.

Then, a time comes when we would avail ourselves of choice, and so have a practical knowledge of the two principles involved. We would know, from personal experience, what is the effect of an actual choice of good and bad upon our personal welfare; how we feel as personal and responsible actors in the drama of life, — still other important informations.

Suppose, now, we choose the bad. It will be evident that we have outraged the authority of morals. It will be apparent, too, that we have weakened the power of choice, by as much as we have set at naught the sanction of morals. For if the latter is contemned, the mischief of the vicious appreciation will appear in the former.

Bear in mind that I am not making a distinction between the power and right of choice, for both are seen in an act of choice, even as both are weakened, whenever the righteous sway of morals is substituted by the domination of the passions; for, constituted as we are, one or the other of these latter must rule.

However this may be, let me repeat that no man can have any real freedom of choice who lightly holds the authority of morals. Choice is always weakened, if not exterminated, when put to playing the artful dodger between right and wrong. If it would hold its own, it should cleave to the right, not solely because it is right, but also because it would be free, — as I shall endeavor to explain.

It has been already remarked that the whole problem of conduct is a matter for the careful appreciations of thought. If, then, we should discover the fact that the sanctity of rectitude should be held inviolable, not solely for reasons of morals, but for those of choice as well; and if we should conclude that this information, if acted on, will secure us both moral good and free choice, in a measure adequate to satisfy the demands of our nobler humanities, then the power to choose between right and wrong can neither derogate from morals nor from the freest choice. And now, if we can attain unto this mount of knowledge, and consistently abide in it, as our rule of conduct, we shall have discovered a way to establish both choice and morals, on an immovable foundation: we shall be free to choose the good.

If any one would object that the habitual observance of the law for rectitude may abridge the freedom of choice, seeing it would practically inhibit choice of sin, let him observe that, in every act of moral choice, we are in effect choosing between good and bad, and so cannot choose the former without comparing it with the latter in order to our preference.

Suppose, though, we do retrench the sweep of choice in the direction of the experiential immoralities, we are certainly not retrenching the sweep of judgment and wise discretion; and if these latter lead us to turn away permanently from sin, then, surely, inasmuch as we have repulsed it for reasons of judicious choice, we have been fortifying the authority of morals whilst extending its sweep in the direction of our higher humanities. But, on the other hand, if we permit us an unlimited indulgence in sin, the sweep of choice will be similarly retrenched in the direction of morals, if not altogether supplanted by the conquering hosts of unbridled lusts.

Here allow another word, *per contra:* We may say of the good man that he is constantly approximating a condition of moral power, wherein he can eschew the bad for inhibitory reasons far surpassing those of the bad man, not simply because of his better appreciation of morals, but because he has a truer estimate of the intrinsic repulsiveness of sin.

An immoral choice deforms both choice and morals. The crushing facts gleam upon us from every new vista in our pathway.

Behold the process, for a moment. Righteousness and sin have been deliberately affirmed as contrasting alternatives. Before us is an act to be done, and there can be no question of our ability to do it. The whole problem of right and wrong is up before us; and we are careful not to act hastily, for we would see to it that we make a judicious choice between the two. And so the choice is made, and we side with the wrong. Right is outraged, and her authority contemned. She may, nevertheless, continue the struggle, chasing the outrage with the painful repressions of remorse. She inflicts a penalty for disloyalty, and in order to a possible reformation. But an authority, once contemned, is, to that extent, crippled. It is to be remarked, however, that, in all this struggle, conscience is but making an effort to uphold the sanctity of right by proper reformatory methods, but without ever challenging the right to choose good or bad, in any one who has still any, the least remnant of it remaining.   And this seems plain.

And, therefore, whenever we are in a position to affirm that a bad choice shall not go unpunished. we are calling attention to the fact that we are neither adequately free, nor completely human, save as we conform to that law of rectitude which conditions true freedom on a judicious and conscientious choice.   And, as bound by that law, it behooves us to see to it that we effect some conception of right, or duty, if we would ever have a self-respecting regard for ourselves.   And, if we would have perfect freedom, we should walk blameless in the law which has in charge the conative aspects and retributions of morals.

For, here and nowhere else, is real freedom of choice.   A violated law tells its own tale of humiliation and ruin.   The sentence of death is already, and ineffaceably, jotted down in the creative act which guards the sanctity of right, by the revenges which follow its violation.

V

We are still in the shadow of a partial overthrow of the supremacy of choice, noting developments. Now, as ever, we act on reasons.   The sinfulness of every desire that besets us has received its every content of power and character through the active intervention of mind.   For what is such a desire (and I may include the propensities on which the desire may be founded) but our thought gazing at some object with an intensity of emotion that voices the potency of our reasons?

It is to be understood that we take the propensities, at any moment on hand to a present thought, as under charge of that thought, and to be dealt with as it deals with any of our common sensations. For, like the latter, they contribute a peculiar batch of characters, of which thought may make use in reaching a decisive choice.

Some may be sinful because we now conceive the sin; others, because we have done so aforetime, and sin sticks.

We may, however, still choose, though on account of our frequent dallying with sin, we now make choice from the lower level of a depraved outlook; our moral powers undergoing a declension uniform with the grade of our turpitude. For, once tampering with sin, we may so foster the mob of unregenerate desires that their importunities may begin to have the force of overmastering demands. And then the power of choice is shattered, and though we may still affect its exercise, we shall be but parading in the dilapidated toggery of a fallen empire.

Nevertheless, if thought is not utterly vanquished, this right of choice, now so abused and battered, has a valid claim in the court of conscience, and so may even yet regain its normal supremacy.

VI

Here the question suggests itself, can mind lose the right of choice utterly, even though sinful de-

sires be persistently cultivated to the last extreme
of beastly excess?

If one be thrown headlong down a precipice, the
propulsion is much more forceful and mechanical
than rational. So of a reckless indulgence in sin.
In this case, to revert to a previous illustration,
the appeal is much stronger than a presbyterial
overture. For, here, the overturists directly antagonize, and finally displace, the authority of the
synod. And we need not add that this fate, not
seldom, betokens the fall of the authority of reason
and conscience.

How then shall we interpret this palpable overthrow of moral choice?

We do not see that a soul ever becomes a slave
to passions, either through some unaccountable
eccentricity of his desires, propensities, or ever
hereditary bent, or, for that matter, anything not
himself, or, at least, not of his own procurement.
The man himself is the author of his own undoing.
He might have controlled his sinful impulsions,
but he did not do it.

In other paragraphs, I availed myself of the
privilege of witnessing him acquiring knowledge
from all quarters, and then adventuring many per-
formances through its power; and I made up my
mind that he could have such desires as came of
his own procurement; and act with clear vision of
his personal responsibility for all he did, or could
do. And, I endeavored to show that he had his
desires made over to him by right of discovery,
just as he got the thoughts that inspired them.

And so, with such views, and feeling, as I did, that he framed every conception of sin and, therefore, of the objects of sinful desires as well, I was not surprised to find him devising a way to secure those objects. And I remarked, further, that as between a sinful inclination thus conceived and fostered, and the object desired, he had deliberately and actually preferred to commit the sin, and so made himself personally responsible for its commission. For, did he not take abundant care to secure this advanced order of personal motives, emotional, desiderative, and voluntary, and to train them to the office of moral factors, on deliberation and purpose, for his own behoof? And does he not take abundant pains to sate them with the very satisfactions he *prefers?*

And now, if he thus deliberately prefer sin, and act on his preference, the act is his own, and he alone is responsible. For, he has walked in the power of thoughts, which awoke him to a knowledge of the voluntary and responsible impulsions due to his human nature.

But it is well to remember, in passing, that there is one thing beyond the power of thought at the command of man. Be his thought what it may, *he has to defer to the inevitable* REVENGES *which follow his sinful indulgences.* He can by no means debauch his moral standards without losing the legitimate control of his emotions and desires, the power of choice and morals undergoing an equal declension and final breakdown. In other words, there is an inability of will, as perhaps Jonathan Edwards put it, but as I would rather have it: The legitimate control of our moral conceptions is frittered away and lost by a base profanation of their divine sanctions. But, Jonathan Edwards aside, once lost, there is never more appeal to reason; the self-assertion and now frenzied aberration of the passions allowing none.

At this stage of my argument, it must be evident to the reader that I do not regard the action of our normal desires or even propensities, supposing they are under the discipline of thought, as presenting to conduct any illicit or unholy instigation which it cannot control. On the contrary, so long as reason retains a shred of conservatism, it inspires and puts its now (let us suppose) somewhat emasculated power into every desire realized in our practical experiences, and to that extent is free.

But, when it abdicates their control, the principle of freedom of choice is either partially or totally nullified. For when we enter upon a career of sinful practices, we may contract bad habits, and then the delirium of the passions may snatch the reins from the nerveless grasp of the intellect, and death burst upon the scene.

If one gives way habitually to sinister influences, he is courting the final overthrow of moral principles. It is only when our moral convictions are held as a dominant power, fearfully ours, and calling upon us to maintain their sway over conduct, that they become our rule of conduct. For, the more habitually one defers to the right, the more he has of true freedom. But suppose, now, that

Q

we have once gone into sin, do we not see that the normal force of our moral convictions is no longer so within our grasp that we can have either the joy or strength that comes to one who has walked in all the ordinances of moral freedom, undefiled ? But, if we weaken the authority of right, we shall so confuse, or else efface the very idea of moral freedom that we shall lose the capacity to appraise our moral conceptions, and so keep in touch with our truer humanities and truer freedom.   Liberty, amended by a profane tampering with its sanctions, is fettered in chains.   And moral choice is confined within limits, beyond which it may not pass, without danger of serious breakage.

To be truly free is to have our freedom in hand, without flaw, or lapse, or declension of any kind. One must welcome the austere authority of right, let it retrench the bastard liberties of the evil-doer ever so much.

The liberty that comes of a monster craze of the passions ends in death.

VII

So then, it comes to this : One cannot have a full measure of freedom without a law to enforce personal responsibility, upon its violation; and if this law be overborne by the despotism of unbridled passions, we are really worse than brutes, wantoning in excesses, without a thought of constraint; we are libertines, sensualists, voluptuaries, with the vulture of remorse preying upon our vitals.

Now, how can we account for all this self-inflicted

ruin, so mournfully prevalent? We may say that there is an inherent proclivity in our very nature, to seek a wilder liberty, through an infraction of its underlying principles.

We may lack faith in our moral convictions, albeit we may never doubt their promise of good to such as walk in their ordinances. For the realization of a promise is projected into the future, and our frail faith may suppress its power; and, lo, we turn away to seek happiness in sinful excesses of the present! This is the liberty of license and death.

But why should it end in a banquet of death? Here I confess to a fear that, notwithstanding the careful presentation of my views, the young reader may see nothing but a vast horde of vile propensities going forth, of their own motion and force, to finish with, and disarm, the power of morals. But I would have him remember that these very propensities, apparently so inimical to morals and freedom (and whatever may be their native force and mission), cannot, at all, act without the cognitive surveillance of mind, and do not act upon *conduct*, unless as trained potencies, and as much our own potencies as any power of thought, or any power consciously achieved by thought; and if so, we have brought upon ourselves the desolations complained of.

Intrinsically, as I have said, the power of moral convictions is stronger than any others, and should have precedence without question, and if we defer to it habitually, we shall know of the power of God and be blessed. But then, in order to our freedom and moral responsibility, just as soon as we can distinguish between right and wrong, we have an alternative choice, and can prefer even the baser than beastly gratifications which end in death; for this seems to be the constitutive and fundamental law for this order of transformations. Indeed, so intent may we be upon some proximate sinful indulgence, and the process of moral dwarfing is so subtile and insidious that we may not feel the shackles we are forging until too late. But this is as much as to say: There is something originally tempting in sin, otherwise we had never made up our mind to it with its lengthening train of pains and penalties.

The truth is that it could never, at all, become an object of choice, if it were so totally repulsive to our fairer and truer humanities that we could not feel inclined to it for reasons of choice, seductively and deliberately immoral, seeing it is an alternative we are not driven to choose in defiance of reason of preference.

VIII

How, then, did we ever come to have this power to choose between right and wrong?

This is an old, old problem, concerning which this paper shall offer no bold teaching. All one can look for is a candid expression of views, within the pale of finite reason.

True, I cannot see with the eyes of Omniscience, but I may see a valid reason for permitting the rise of sin under a dispensation which provides for a moral government coupled with pains and penalties, and connected with a plan of salvation which exalts the true believer even above the angels.

And allow me to say that, although this plan is complicated with the question of eternal punishment, I think I can see why even such frail creatures as we are — always excepting such witless and godless humanitarians as take it upon themselves to go before the Omniscient as an emergency force, to soften the rigor of eternal justice — why even such creatures as we are would not hesitate to rise, as one man, and demand the limitless punishment, and even extinction, of a class of obdurate criminals whom it were impossible to deter from trampling upon the principles of purity and social rectitude upon which the very life of our common humanity rests.

But the ultimate reason why sin and death came into the world no man can tell. Omniscient thought and righteousness alone can answer that question. But why should we stumble at the mystery, at least, so long as we are not permitted to have an all-comprehensive vision of the universe?

Outside nature has a rock-ribbed scheme of transformations peculiar to herself. The vegetable and animal kingdoms have each a several scheme distinct from the former, so also has man one uniquely his own. And no man can understand *either* thoroughly. How unspeakably unjust, then, would it be to compare these diverse works to the disadvantage of either? Who can compare the poet Keats with

Achilles or Ajax? Who has the psychological ability to compare mind with mere physical power?

Still, two paintings may be compared in respect of their fidelity to nature, and we may see that one will surpass the other, for we are comparing works of one man with another's. But now let us conceive a painter of diviner vision than any other man. He has for motive-subject, let us imagine, the sea, and its wild rolling waves. The painter's vision is away off into the illimitable distances. The perceptive appreciations of his eye surpassing those of any ordinary man, it would be quite natural for him to depict a coloration of waves at great distances quite different from the dark, deep, sea-green plastering seen in our best canvases. Indeed, the characteristic positions and curves peculiar to the shifting and blending of the fluctuations might be caught up and rendered with a degree of truth, literally bewildering to outsiders. But whether a superior power of perspective could accomplish this, I know not, for I am not a painter.

Now what would be the judgment of contemporary artists on such a picture? Not seeing nature, as he saw it, they would pounce upon it as a sheer perversion of her actual look, a wanton spoliation of her features. Whereas, in fact, he alone would be giving us a bit of nature, a picture truer to nature, but not to be seen with our imperfect eyes.

It is readily seen that, with shortened visual apperceptions, and denser perspective insight, the adverse criticism could never be justified. It takes a higher order of mind to pass upon a higher order of work.

CHAPTER XX

ALTERNATIVE CHOICE

I

THIS problem is difficult. The sturdiest thinker may not solve it. It should have careful thought and fair treatment. Du Bois-Reymond shall begin the argument: "That in a given instant one or the other of two things will happen is unthinkable," says he. I enter no dissent, not seeing where the trouble comes in. For, taking thought to be free is no reason, so far as I can see, why its acts of choice are so ordered that "in a given instant one *or* the other of two things will happen," or that either shall happen irrespective of a rational preference of one. Reasons lay hold of "one," and cast out "the other": Reasons determine choice. No reasons, no choice; no "one" and no "other."

And choice is a rational preference of "one," on information which forbids our selecting "the other"; not the indifference of an idiot, flitting heedlessly from one thing to another. It is the absolute negation of rational indifference, and means that we are acting on some final reason for preferring "one of two things." We prefer the one and reject the other, until we see a reason for a change of conviction. The stronger reason will forever displace

a weaker. So, whenever we have this stronger reason, we have our choice, or rational preference, and,
along with this, a righteous personal responsibility.

When, therefore, we choose the "one," we reject
"the other," by a rational preference and rejection,
not because, for example, we can taste apple and
peach, and then take either, ignoring the difference,
without concern, wish, or aversion, as between the
two. The force of some reason or information, in
accordance with which we cleave to one of two
alternatives, determines our partiality, or preference for it. The person as responsible, is as much
in every act of choice, as in every act of thought.

And so, it is indeed "unthinkable" for one who
acts on choice to stride from one to the other,
whilst holding to one, without making any difference. The act of choice *confines* him to the chosen
alternative, at the "instant" of choice.

The result is that, if choice of the one is a rejection of the other, then, every such choice is a
rational discrimination, and preference, which pre-
cludes our choosing the latter in the self-same
instant we are holding to the former.

If we make choice at all, we shall have to stand
upon our prevailing reason, and a prevailing reason
cannot be prevailed against. Indeed, we cannot
rise to a full act of choice, until the power of some
prevailing reason comes in to complete our choice.

II

But my position may be apprehended the better,
if set forth in the lines of some conclusions reached

in previous discussions. This I will presently offer to do.

Thought secures choice. Having thought, we have a reason for choice, and act upon our reason; that is to say, we prefer, or choose, in accordance with our cognitive intimations, and so, if we are free, we are beholden to some power of our thought, and not to an alien force.

If these views are correct, it is evident that choice is not free (indeed is not anything), in the sense of being independent of motives or reasons, but acts *through* their *power;* and that this power, whether manifested in emotions or desires, or otherwise traced back to pure intellections, is the energy that goes finally into conduct and deeds. We are beholden to our own efforts, for any knowledge we ever have, searching for and appropriating our finds; and that knowledge alone is our causal efficient, ours and free, because, having acquired it discursively, we can make use of it conatively, free from causal constraint *ab extra.*

Then again, choice must not, indeed cannot, be made over to us by any exterior agency. It must come, if at all, through the informations we have been at pains to work for, or more correctly, through the one we have decisive reasons for acting on. For, unless I acquire the power to discriminate between two competing alternatives, and to elect one, how can I take to it by a rational preference, or on the other hand, reject the other, by a positive, tangible affirmation of its ineligible traits?

To do, or not to do, one or the other of two things

is decided by an act of judgment affirming prefer-ence, and therefore precluding the motiveless flop-ping about from one to the other alternative, of course with variations quite "unthinkable" and innumerable.

The power of a final reason explodes in a selective restriction to one. And this power, let me repeat, being ours by right of intelligent acquisition, is, hence, equally ours, when employed in committing us to a line of conduct which we have chosen, and for which we hold ourselves personally responsible.

And, therefore, would I emend Du Bois-Rey-mond's dictum, so as to have it read: "That in a given instant one or the other of two things will happen" (*in defiance of a prevailing reason*) "is unthinkable." This lets in the facts which cover the case, giving the proper (selective) power of the decisive word in acts of choice, to the agency which has been to the trouble, both to discover the alter-natives, and the reasons for choice, between them. And this is all I claim for it. Choice, then, is a rational preference. And so, indeed, a non-rational choice is inconceivable. The power of some deci-sive thought must be present, to commit us per-sonally to acts for which we are consciously and personally responsible.

III

Here an objector presents his view: "We grant all you say, still, how could one choose either of two alternatives, without being led to his choice either by his character or precedent reasons?

For answer to this I remark: 1. We make our character what it is by discovering the informations that determine its nature, mission, and value, and have thus made it ours by force of the thoughts that went to equip it for the work of choice.

2. Having thus acquired all the informations that can be construed as in any way efficient in attempering choice, we have acquired the right to employ them as our own, whether acquired now, or at any previous time. So then, it comes to this: If we have a present reason, free by right of intelligent discovery, how can it be under bondage to those previously acquired in order to it, and likewise free by the same right? The precedent and present reasons are equally free, and equally ours, by the same right of discovery. In other words, we have both character and choice, through the informations which go to make them what they are, and to make them ours, to be used as our own.

Our antecedent acquisitions stand to the subsequent ones as enabling attainments, much like educational advantages to children, qualifying them for thinking and acting for themselves. For, when children act from native impulses, and without the guidance of thought, the impulses are everything, and the actors nothing but puppets played upon by powers not their own. But when taught of the ideas they have achieved, they have educated potentials in hand for determining choice and conduct, and so become responsible actors; acting and responsible by reason of informations, whether acquired in the present, or at any other time.

IV

I note, in passing, some other distinctions. Choice must be of something allowable. On the way to its last stage, it is either alterable, or unalterable. We are often, for a season, as much purposed to choose one alternative as another; for we may be making our way in doubt. Still, we are never wholly indifferent in the presence of our alternatives.

We are not to suppose, however, that every opinion is open to change. Some have our unchangeable assent. An endless stream of changes would secure neither certainty nor stability, and choice would be futile, vanishing utterly in a flux of consecutions without result.

Contrariwise, the search for a definitive choice is a quest for something definite and certain, a search for an access of discursive power, sufficient for a chosen result. For we are battling for a teleological find, and must take thought, in view of the personal ends and interests at stake.

The first important step we take is to conceive and outline our competing and contrasting alternatives. Then follow many tentative conceptions as to their eligibility, or ineligibility, in respect of what we shall do with ourselves and things not ourselves, etc., etc. All this to prelude what follows.

Necessitarians assume that, if allowed to choose, we are at the mercy of shoreless uncertainties, but if we have certainty, we are in the jaws of necessity. I enter here a general and particular

denial of both assumptions. I shall remark first
upon the argument from uncertainties, confining
my attention, for the present, mainly to what pre-
cedes and prepares for the coming out of choice.

To begin with, let us believe that we have to
wrestle with a world of uncertainties. We are not
self-luminous, neither are we filled with all knowledge from start to finish. We have to cleave our
way, as best we can, to certainties, resting on the
evidences for the facts, which we can affirm and
act upon. Furthermore, we are impelled to elabo-
rate, and hold to, opinions, on consideration of the
evidences for them, — because we would not have
them (indeed they cannot be) thrust upon us, in
defiance of our consent, but would rather have them
discovered and wrought up by cognitive methods
which attest our judgment, and put us on the road
to choice and responsibility, where we can act as
we think. For, when one acts discursively, he
becomes personally implicated in solving the problems on which he acts; asserting powers of his
own, and struggling for more.

The opinion on which we act may be one of a
thousand, and may hang on the brink of disaster
a thousand times. At one moment, it may be
supreme, at another, crowded aside by others, and
so on, *ad infinitum.*

Often, the leading points of the best matured
plans have to be abandoned, and often, again, important decisions annulled, the check to our policy becoming absolute. We may be a nation struggling
for supremacy on land and water. If we adhere to

old wont and custom, we may encourage our rivals by proofs of weakness, irresolution, etc. And, thereupon, we resolve to disenchant them, lest, peradventure, we invite assault, when least prepared for it.

That this nice balancing of views results in a corresponding vacillation of purpose is evident. But in all this shifting of position, we are but taxing the mind's distinctive resources to arrive at certainty of choice and action. And, if so be we reach a conclusion exact to these requirements, we have gained our point. We have reached a decision that goes forth into result as a voluntary certainty springing from the power of thought. We have seen our way to a cognitive result, and cannot longer dally with the uncertainties we were aforetime eliminating.

And now, the world has an indubitable certainty, modulated into conformity to our thoughts.

Here I interpose a passing remark: The uncertainties, referred to above, arise, not so much from the sheer difficulty of reaching a *certain* conclusion (anybody of the ordinary sort can have such by the thousands), as from the fact that we may not feel *bound* to *act on* even the correctest conclusion, seeing we can choose moral good or bad, on condition of personal responsibility for our choice. And so, we have a very common uncertainty which arises from the fact that, for reasons of choice, we accommodate opinion to the cry of our degraded propensities and sinful habits.

I am not now to discuss morals. I am simply

claiming that all these, and other, uncertainties, at least so far as they help us on the way to choice and action, are the characteristic features of a free cause, as contradistinguished from either a necessitating one, or an alleged power to choose any alternative, irrespective of a prevailing reason. And, therefore, is it evident that, so far from clashing with the prerogatives of choice, they are in order to its discovery and command of its own multitudinous rational certainties, opening the way to a chosen result. And in so doing, thought has gone to the trouble of placing within the pale of fact and reality a whole class of certainties, rational and voluntary, unknown to and beyond the reach of blind material transformations, for they are not mechanical results, but discursive achievements born of thought.

What is of nature, belongs to nature, what of thought, to thought. The diversities of the two can never be commuted, and never equated. The essential certainties, for the thoughtful and responsible factor, are a prevailing reason and the choice which is born with and founds on that reason.

I explain further. Thought seeking reasons why it should, or should not, pursue a given line of conduct, is quite a different thing from what it is when in an act of choice and performance. In the former, though we may form any number of wavering, but valid, opinions, we may not see our way to choice, with absolute certainty. In the latter, we stand upon a finality, the power of thought giving us a chosen result. Whether the difficulty of prediction obtains equally in things material is not within the scope of our present inquiry. What is uncertain for any reason is so, only because it is unknown. And, whether there is as much, or more of it, in the one case as in the other, I do not know, and do not care to know. A voluntary cause is sufficient unto itself, by a law of thought which discovers its own certainties, and which permits and conditions choice and personal responsibility, on the presence of a prevailing reason.

Such a discursive cause may have to make the acquaintance of uncertainties innumerable. But then, its mission is to take charge of these uncertainties, and carefully labor up to conclusions on which it may act decisively. And in all this, it is a discoverer and revealer of a transformed and transcendent order of facts denied to any form or combination of matter which cannot act on its reasons (if it have any). But such uncertainties as are gone upon in view of results are part and parcel of every problem of morals and conduct brought before a competent intelligence.

The measure of all certainty is thought and its rational standards, and if this is so, it will be at pains to guard against any uncertainty of choice between two alternatives. It has discovered a knowledge, say, of the sequences of material causation, and communes with these as evidencing some trace of creative intelligence left in that work. It remarks that no event can take place independent of some law of thought to safeguard its advent. For, if anything could come at the call of utter lawlessness, the whole scheme of mind, power, and action, for man, would fall to the ground.

Thought discovers and acts upon some law of thought in all it does. When the merchants of New York would ship goods to the Great West, we do not find they go by the way of Spitzbergen or the Amazon. A discursive law of some kind is forever on the watch against such a peripatetic diversion. Everything, everywhere, acts as it is, or has been, informed by some inviolable behest of thought. And here, I need not say that matter is so bound by the law for material sequences that it has no action of its own, and no power to determine any. Thought, too, has to conform to the fundamental laws of its creation, in virtue of which it has been left free to determine actions of its own by powers of its own. And, now, because it is an innovating, constructive, cognitive force, with power to act on the informations it achieves, its task is to win a fresh wealth of verities, utterly unknown in the realm of material transformations.

For example, the natural walk of electricity is necessitated. As conditioned by natural limitations, it can never press forward into the new combinations so recently sought out by scientists. So, also, in the manufacture of metals, we may remark a number of chemical reactions taking place at the command of, and in accordance with, some requirement of thought.

A rational certainty is, then, not one of this cast-iron sort, but has to be elaborated, and integrated by some present effort of thought.

R

And for this reason, we may not predict every discursive event with absolute certainty. But if we could, where would be the need of choice, seeing we could, then, have our own, and our neighbor's, actions consciously affirmed in the present?

Indeed, if we could antecedently trump up acts still in the future, and still depending on future inclinations to good or bad, this exhaustive sweep of prediction would be omniscient. Moreover, an unlimited power of forecasting results among men, would, in practice, amount to a thoroughgoing communism of intellects absolutely identical and omniscient. But if we are to be free, and individually responsible, we have at our command a power of rational discursion and research which will provide the world with an order of certainties and acts born of our individual thoughts. And yet it is a distinguishing trait of an agent, individually thoughtful, that, whilst his acts may be logically certain (and when gone upon, logically determined *certainties*), they may never be foreknown with absolute certainty; unless, perhaps, you could identify your mind with your neighbor's, and also anticipate every turn of thought, and every extraneous circumstance of the future.

V

So far, we have not seen the shadow of the faintest resemblance of necessity in acts of choice. But a new horror flits across the stage!

It is objected that when choice becomes unchangeable and certain, it is because of the reasons which constrain and compel us to make it. Now, we might admit all this constraint, etc., and then deny that the force of our reasons, be they ever so stringent, can militate against our freedom of choice. We do admit that the march of thought is onward and irresistible. For we are so tied down to our reasons that we cannot break with them. Our choice is for reasons so invincibly ours, that we cannot take sides against them, without taking sides against ourselves. Their power is our own. We have, first, the force of the thoughts we have achieved, and, then, their consummation in choice, as result.

However, let us now have a fair exhibit of the quality and intent of their peculiar constraint. And here it is pertinent to inquire, how we ever came to have alternatives before us, competing for preference? Observe two ordinary ones. How did they become such? Only through the power of some thought of ours, placing them in contrast. As alternatives, they have neither power, nor existence even, except what we have given them in the act of conception that parts them off into contrasted, but elective, constituents, for the exercise of a discriminating partiality.

Now then, inasmuch as we cannot constrain ourselves by our own powers, — for all such pressure must have our own consent, and would therefore be our own, and not that of an exterior force, — the question of constraint is resolved into one of *consent*, determined by our reasons, and therefore devoid of the least taint of necessity, in the ordinary acceptation of the term. And so, we have the alternatives of choice, with their quality and *quantum* of power, made such by the conceptive and constructive efficiency of mind; made what we would have them to be, in power, pressure, or constraint.

VI

Consider, now, what takes place in an act of choice.

We have just made our alternatives available in an act of conception. And, now, if we make choice of either, we must conceive a reason for it. So, we compare the one with the other, in order to ascertain which is the more eligible. We are in quest of informations on which to act; informations, whose special power we employ when we prefer (choose) one thing and reject another.

Remember, we had to resort to reasons for setting up the sign of alternative choice in our mind. And now, we would have reasons for coming to an actual choice, preferring one thing to the other.

Here my argument is that this sign of eligible alternatives previously set up in our minds, as above stated, does, in fact, suggest (orient) alternative action; and, if we act on the suggestion and make choice, we are but giving reality to one of the eligible constituents of our alternative conception. We end, as we start. Completed choice is conception realized; and this, in turn, is but to realize, or give a practical issue to, the force, pressure, or *constraint* of our conceptions, — on choice, preference, or consent.

VII

It is further objected that the very force of our convictions so fastens choice to one of the alternatives that we are disabled from choosing the other, and that, therefore, there is, after all, no such thing as a free alternative choice.

This objection, whatever else it may mean, implies that a free choice calls for certain indefinable and unfathomable, voluntary variations taking place in defiance of reason and judgment. This would certainly be very "unthinkable."

Among a certain class of theorists, there seems to be a vague notion that a free cause should be made of anything that comes handy. But, let such advanced thinkers try their hand at giving us their definition of a will, *minus* a prevailing reason charged with the proper efficiency for determining acts. Of course, there can be no acts of any kind without power of some kind to produce them. But the very moment they would equip such a handy cause with power to act, this pretentious argument, from a *forceful* vigor of reasons to necessity, or, if you prefer, from the absence of a prevailing reason to a free cause or free determination, would fall to the ground.

As a matter of fact, consciously affirmed in all manner of discursions, we get the opinion we want, and put it to work, where we want; going with it, where we want it to go; and it has the precise amount, and kind, of power, we want it to have, and no other.

For, whatever the opinion may be on which we act, it, and its power, or pressure, is ours by right of conception, preference, and conation, and, when we make choice, it does not mean that our opinion can be emptied of its power, and, evasively and indifferently, make for any alternative.

If we choose at all, it must be for sufficient reasons, and if so be we acquire these, we have acquired the power to choose and act. Constraint, or bondage, coming from an appreciative discrimination of our own select alternatives, is a self-contradiction. Our thought, as causative, is but the force of our reasons, as active. And, if nothing but this, the pressure is of our own procurement, that is to say, by virtue of intelligent elaboration.

But, perhaps, a simpler way of testing this general theory of constraint, or compulsion, would be a brief contrast of our own powers with powers not our own.

You bid a servant to do this or that! He obeys, *with consent and on reflection*. And so, the determination is his own and therefore free, by right of consent. But, he may disobey, for good reasons. In this, too, he is free from bondage to opinions not his own, for he held fast to his own, and disobeyed. But now, if he obey under pressure from his neighbor, he would be a slave. And the same is true of any exterior force overriding one's reasons. It would be a case of bondage, compulsion, necessity, etc.

But freedom to choose enables the chooser to compass his ends by the power of his own thoughts;

his acts responding to the call (here power) of some decisive conviction. Our causality is an act of consent, or choice.

We may here ponder another illustration. If, in the existing order of things, all the resources of thinking had been committed to a select few, who, having thus a monopoly of ideas, apportioned them out among the ignorant rabble, then, these latter might rightfully complain of bondage to ideas not their own, and because not their own. And yet, notwithstanding all this intellectual despotism, if the masses themselves were still free to conceive it to be for their good, they would be free, to that extent.

And so, from every point of view, the conclusion is irresistible that the acts of a free agent can have neither existence nor power, except so far as he has power of thought to decide upon them. How, then, can anything exterior come in, as an interloper, between our thought and its power, at least so long as we are permitted to do our own thinking?

What we have through mind must have our sanction, for it comes at our call, and so, is free.

We may constrain other things, but can never constrain a thought, or be constrained, or necessitated, by one. Consider what takes place in moving an arm. Thought is both cognitive and actile, or conative, with no intermediary between it and what it does. The act is its own, and, therefore, free. True, we avail ourselves of bone, muscle, nerves, etc., instrumentalities furnished of God. But, as previously explained, so far as we can take advantage of furnished materials coming from any source whatever, they certainly do not unfit us for exercising our voluntary powers upon them.

When America was discovered, the aborigines knew nothing of iron. The more thoughtful Spaniard brought it over. The Indian picked it up, and used it. Did the iron, thus furnished, abridge his freedom, any more than the copper with which he had furnished himself, ages before the advent of the Spaniard ? Was he any freer without it ?

At all events, the use we make of our arms or limbs does not estop, or hinder, or conflict with our discursive freedom in the least particular. To put our power on things exterior to our thought, even to constrain them to serve our purposes, is a plain vindication of the several power of mind. And, to take that step, we must acquire a fit knowledge of them, and what we can do with them. In other words, we make up our mind that we can employ them to our advantage, and then act in pursuance of our thought, doing what we prefer doing.

Now, to apply this line of remarks to the subject in hand, we maintain that, although man may constrain other things to his purposes, he may never, at all, constrain, or be constrained by, his own thoughts. He is very careful to work up to the complexity of the task before him, but ever with a view to actualizing his thoughts. And so, the question is, not that he can make use of other things, but whether he can have an opinion of his own and take advantage of it, be it what it may, and exercised on what it may.

VIII

And now I would have a last word or two with the logicians. I have no unkindness for logic of the veracious sort. But when plain facts contradict nineteenth-century, syllogistic reasoning, I may be fairly excused for losing faith in the argument for necessity stated in that traditional form. I give it in full: —

    1. Every change is caused.
        A volition is a change.
        It is, therefore, caused.

    2. What is caused, is necessitated.
        A volition is caused.
        It is, therefore, necessitated.

And now for our animadversions! The major premise of the second syllogism (what is caused, is necessitated) is neither an axiomatic, nor universal, truth. It is no truth at all. It is a palpable perversion of fact, a *suppressio veri*. But facts, alone, should determine the contents of our syllogisms. For, if not informed by these, they cannot be tolerated in any court of reason. What is needed, is not a regulation form of words, but a plain statement in any words that will carry the facts.

I own that my views call in question the so-called universal law of causation, a law which has dominated and crazed logic from time immemorial. I deny that this law can embrace the universe of *mind*. Nor is there any conceivable reason why

it should.   A law of causation, universal for matter, is all right.   And a law of causation, universal
for mind, is equally right.   No one need disturb
either.   And there is no reason why anything,
under heaven, should disturb either law, least of
all should a law of matter overstep its plain limitations, and displace one peculiar to mind.   It
would be just as reasonable to contend that a law
for discursion and choice displaces the law of gravitation.   However that may be, there seems to be,
nowadays, a widely prevalent feeling, a relic of the
a priori teachings, that a law is in better form,
or, at least, a better law, if you give it a wide extension; the wider, the better.   Remark the general tendency to discover the universal law.   From
time immemorial we meet with these all-comprehending universals.   There is the universal (?) law
of gravitation.   But does that law apply to *mind*,
or I might say, to electricity and the luminiferous
ether?   Pray, tell me, if either of the above is
ponderable.   Besides, illustrations drawn from what
matter is and does, are utterly valueless for the
interpretation of the self-conscious cognitions and
transformations of mind, to say nothing of electricity and the luminiferous ether, neither of which, so
far as I can see, are either mind or matter.   It may
seem strange, but is yet a fact, that everything in
the universe is privileged, by common consent, to
have its peculiar class of powers for doing its
peculiar kind of work, — except thought.   But
why should it be contraband?   Why should it not
be free to hold a court of discursion, judgment, and

choice, and manage its own affairs, in its own way?

It has certainly a history, not to say a folk-lore, of its own, along with that of causation; and no law of material causation has ever dared to say nay to its acquiring informations, and consequently power specially qualified to command a result in accordance with the distinctly discursive methods which furnish us with deeds, or acts, for which we are personally responsible. But in order to an even-handed discussion with necessitarians of the syllogistic camp, I construct a pair of syllogisms which, let us hope, have some respect for facts.

1. What is voluntarily caused, affirms the voluntary power of the antecedent. A volition is voluntarily caused. Therefore it affirms the voluntary power of its antecedent.

2. What is accomplished by the power of a sufficient reason, is a voluntary act or free achievement. An act of choice is thus accomplished. It is, therefore, a voluntary act or free achievement.

These syllogisms will be referred to, and explained in connection as we proceed. You are careful to notice that I am recognizing the fact that, when a cognitive cause passes on to result, the latter is the final stage of the former. A peculiar cause will forever give a peculiar result, let a law for material causation be what it may. For example: Two men at work on the same subject-matter will reach results as characteristically dissimilar as their dissimilar casts of mind, and the different mental and other training they have undergone. But why? Because each has a power of thought distinctly individual and personal, in respect of quality and vigor. Now, to compare mental and material, or mechanical, power, what forbids the former, as a cause distinctly individual and dissimilar, achieving results characteristically free in contrast with the latter? It has been shown elsewhere that, in any work of mind, its impress may be traced in all we know of that work. The law for uniformity in nature, and diversity of causes, affirms all this when it declares that *like* CAUSES *produce like* RESULTS. And it results, as a consequence from a principle, that *unlike* causes produce *unlike* results.

Indeed, until you allow for the peculiarities of the cause, all you can affirm of any result is that *it is caused,* nothing more. But the question whether it is free or necessitated, even the how and wherefore of its *modus operandi,* lies wholly with the several ability of the antecedent. And, therefore, when thought conceives a result posited *in futuro,* and which it afterward achieves, this result can claim no other antecedent efficient than the volitional one that cognitively achieved it, if it be permitted to give its own version of the details of performance.

Ponder distinctly what we have before us. I need scarcely say, an actor and his act. If he is free in conceiving his act, can any one tell me how he turns up a slave by completing the act? The power seated in his thought has simply moved from the former to the latter, — the completed act only making the transition and transaction the better known, or knowable, as a whole, — giving us the finishing touches to a deed or work, to which we have committed ourselves irrevocably. And, therefore, should our syllogisms be so constructed as to cover these facts.

I repeat: A thought once free, as cause, cannot take up any tinge of necessity from the fact of going on to completion, as result. The same efficiency that conceives completes the result; and so both conception and result are attempered by the voluntary findings and determinations of mind.

That the power of thought may compel or necessitate exterior things by as much as it can modify or control their wonted transformations in the interest of itself has been previously explained; but always in order to accomplishing our purposes, and, therefore, as ancillary to a contemplated result. But, in this case also, our act, taken as the realization of a preceding conception, is but the *intelligent renewal and complete establishment* of the conception whose power went forth to consummate it. As conception, or reason, or motive, or voluntary impulse, it has only assumed a final phase which we agree to name result, or completed choice. For, result must first be conceived, ere it can ever be achieved. And, if so, it is potentially achieved when only conceived; the sole difference being in the stage of action reached, whereby what was once potential is now an active, and actually operative, cause.

And now, allow me to ask, if the mere potential

is free and voluntary, how can it become bond by taking a resolutely decisive step? Would it not be quite as reasonable for one to say it is necessitated, because it is in process of completion, as because it has reached completion?

And here, I should perhaps explain that, as a cognitive result is conceived and gone into on purpose, it will often require a prolonged study to reach a decisive conviction exact for the determination of a satisfactory choice. And therefore again, choice as result from our study, is a personal achievement conceived to be for our good (or bad), etc., and is, therefore, informed of all these particulars of thought; and, if so, then, opinions, motives, volitions, etc., are preëminently achievements of personal power by and for the agent, and, as such, are logically employed in the tasks of free determinations.

So much to clear the way for constructing a syllogism which shall be informed of and conserve the controlling facts of free determinations.

IX

I propose now, to offer a syllogism which, I may hope, will accommodate the facts, and the logic of the facts uncovered in the discussions of the preceding section; for I am not quite done with the false assumptions of these mechanical views of voluntary determinations.

3. Every change that is a conscious renewal, and establishment of the power that conceived it, is a free result.

Motives, opinions, reasons of choice, etc., are a conscious renewal, and establishment of the power that conceived them.

Therefore they are free results.

It will be seen, and I hope the reader will carefully note the fact, that I am here regarding motives, opinions, reasons, etc., for choice, not now as causes going into results when we are ripe for them, but as RESULTS from our previous efforts to achieve them, and therefore determined, or fetched by those previous efforts. For what is born of a previous perceptive, conceptive, analytic, and synthetic elaboration and combination of materials, is the result of those previous efforts.

And surely, any information, or idea on which we may finally act, and here viewed as beholden to some careful, previous pondering, cannot be anything but the conscious renewal and complete establishment of the antecedent competency that went forth to conceive or achieve it. And, therefore, if the antecedent motives, reasons, ends, etc., were likewise achieved by, and for, the same agent, and no matter for what intent, how can the subsequent ones, similarly achieved, and for any purpose, but here taken as *results* from the previous elaboration, conflict in any wise with voluntary determinations, of which they were part and parcel?

You apprehend that I am denying that a law for material causation can, at all, apply to a discursive competency which underlies and informs every act of choice, conceiving and accomplishing what it conceives. But this it could not do, if a law for material causation which claims that "what is caused is necessitated," could foist itself into the body and soul of discursion and supplant or suppress its intelligent procedures.

The act of thinking is the life of mind, and every such act involves the unbroken continuity and identity of that life in every stage of conception and action. And, therefore, is it that mind is a ceaseless discursive flow of free antecedents and consequents. Its condition, at any one instant, is a free achievement in the present projected from a free achievement gone upon in the previous instant, and so on, back to the first thought; a preceding achievement ever combining with and establishing a subsequent one, without the possibility of a split in the discursive fusion, or a break in the continuity. And if this is a true psychology of the mental transformations resorted to, we have here an irreducible unit of discursive power and personal responsibility running back to the beginnings of thought.

And therefore, I lay down the following proposition, as incontrovertible: Man's freedom lies in the sturdy continuity of his discursive methods, whereby thought, at each instant, renews and founds on the competency it had reached in the previous, indivisible instant. And therefore, and in this regard, conception and choice, viewed even as results from previous thoughts, are different from all other results, seeing that they are a continuous renewal and reassertion of the power that achieved them, and not simply receptive of that power, after the manner of results determined by an exterior power.

X

And now I shall ask logicians to make room for another fact.

It is known that each man for himself believes that he determines his own acts freely. Shall an antiquated syllogism which avers that, whatever is caused, is necessitated, be permitted any longer to nullify a rational, universal, and constant deliverance of thought, that man everywhere, and under all circumstances, believes he is free and acts upon his belief? Observe that this conviction is fortified by the undogmatic and non-speculative character of the testimony. It is also further strengthened by the fact that the witnesses affirm their conviction with one accord, and without previous concert, or collusive advisement. Besides, the belief is alike individual, universal, and constant, in the sense that all the individuals who constitute the universal, at all times, and under all circumstances, persist in affirming this belief, none denying it, and none capable of denying it, at least, so long as man thinks and acts for himself. Could any fact be more firmly grounded on evidence?

We are told, though, that such belief, however honestly held, is untutored, illogical, and not to be trusted. Of course, we are thankful that all men, under all circumstances, as long as we can think and act for ourselves on reasons of conscious knowledge and evidence, can persist in *honestly* entertaining a stupid belief in the teeth of such logical teachers. However, if the logic of the evidence is irresistible, no wonder we all have the stupid belief. We can honestly believe, say our sapient logicians! How exceedingly kind and patronizing are our superiors! Still, it may stretch one's sense of conventional courtesy a trifle too much to compliment a chimpanzee for some rudimentary conceptions of an honest, but pitifully illogical sort. However, the chimpanzee has never been taught of the exotic lore of *formal logic*, any more than *all* men.

But if all men, at all times, and under all circumstances, will still persist in maintaining a stupid belief, even after a so-called logical disproof of it, how could it be possible for any set of men, with such hopelessly stolid and illogical antecedents, ever to acquire such knowledge of *formal* logic as to divine what it is to be either logical or illogical?

Voluntary freedom is either a discovery at first hand or an inference from one. We judge it on informations consciously affirmed and carried forward into acts; and if all men affirm these informations, they are affirming voluntary powers, consciously cognitive and, therefore, personal and free. Indeed, if it were so that we had no knowledge of our own powers, but could reason, as we now do, about the actions of other animate creatures, we should be led, logically, and correctly, to infer that they were free to the full extent of their mental capacities.

Formal logic, if true to reason and the evidence, is, and can be, nothing but the statement of, say, the informal cognitions and affirmations, on evidence that justified and built up the individual and universal conviction of human freedom. For such a conviction is attested in affirming every thought and every achievement of thought. In fact, if any belief can be affirmed as true, because affirmed in achieving and affirming our every thought, the belief that we are free to think and act for ourselves, in defiance of the law for material causation, must be accepted as logically validated, on incontrovertible evidence.

If there be such a measure of gullibility and fallacy in this belief of volitional freedom, let our logicians prove either an incorrigible imbecility, or else utter recklessness on the part of all men in respect of the laws of their own thinking. But if we all say that we are free, — spelling out, in all literalness, our conscious thoughts and acts, — an informal but fundamental logic, veraciously accredited beyond the possibility of doubt, will affirm our freedom from what we affirm in every thought, and every phase of thought.

We are not to deny that there are many foolish beliefs; some anthropomorphic, some naturalistic, and some material. Explaining nature too literally from the standpoint of consciousness, we have fetichism. Explaining man in terms of external nature, we have atheism, materialism, and bad logic. Both issue in myth. The former is the first rude attempt, among uncivilized peoples, to reduce the chaos of facts observed in the material world to some rational coherence. The latter is a later stage of this systemizing tendency, but put forth to correct the dismal follies of the former. Indeed, some eminent scientists are even now prating glibly of Darwinian theories which work forward under the guidance of laws which know not a lawgiver.

And here, I would explain that mere science, authority, antiquity, etc., are no conclusive proof of any theory which conflicts with belief in any *fact* at first hand ; to say nothing of a belief consciously affirmed in affirming anything, from a discursive fact within us to any theory, true, or false. For, although men have given way to sundry baseless beliefs, and have stoutly maintained them for ages unnumbered, still, after all that is said, we do not find that all men, at *any time*, have given way to any theory at war with their belief in the fact that they are free to determine their own acts. For a fact, thus consciously affirmed, can never be disturbed by any amount of theorizing about it. Indeed, such a universal belief, so avouched for all men under all circumstances, must be consistent with every belief similarly avouched, and whether of mind or matter, as I have endeavored to explain in preceding paragraphs. And, as to this particular belief in man's freedom, no theory of necessity founded on mechanical causation is at all applicable to a power which determines choice by discursive methods and considerations for which men universally hold themselves responsible.

We have no right to take either mind or matter, thought or sensation, and construct a theory at war with the facts of either. We are not permitted to tamper with our facts.

We must allow for the diversely appointed and

restricted powers of self and not self, if we are to preserve the purity and individuality of their social intercourse intact. Truth is never to be had by disregarding the laws which prescribe and restrict the interaction of entities diversely empowered and individualized.

If you interview matter, you will remark the molecular ring of mechanical transformations issuing from its very pores. On the other hand, if you could but touch pure intellect, you would possibly observe nothing but a gleam of light, pale, pulseless, and chilly cold, streaming forth from the tips of your fingers. But man is more than sheerly intelligent; and so if you interview him, you will discover life, individuality, and personal responsibility,—a discursive energy, innovating, thoughtful, conative, — burning with voluntary impulsions and humanities as bright as his intelligence. Thus far, we are dealing with the facts of matter and mind.

Now, what shall we say of logicians who would give us truth by a mere formal arrangement of words so devised that such facts as our conscious affirmations disclose are either cast away, or driven to the wall.

The logic is with the facts, and not with the select few who propound premises with the facts of our conscious affirmations left out. And yet, if the select few have been all their lives, and are even now, indulging a silly belief of their freedom, they have a poor way of backing their qualifications for reforming that, or any other, belief.

However, to be fair, I offer them the benefit of a

formal syllogism which will cover their distrust of the informal logic of all men.

4. Whoever habitually thinks, and acts on the belief, that he is free, has no conception of the logical connection between the power of thought and free determination.

All men so think and act, and that habitually. They have, therefore, no conception of the logical connection between the power of thought and free determination.

It is pleasant to hope that such a syllogism will allay any distrust of my absolute fairness in dealing with the theoretical and formalizing logicians. Still, one could wish them to give one the logic of incontrovertible *facts ;* for every other kind is chimerical.

But let me now contrast this mendacious syllogism with one which will have a due regard for the facts.

5. A conviction affirmed in affirming every thought and every act of thought is the one true fact of the logical understanding, — equally individual, universal, authoritative, and incontrovertible. The fact that we are free is so affirmed. It is, therefore, the one true fact of the logical understanding, — equally individual, universal, authoritative, and incontrovertible.

XI

I recall, in passing, a point or two touched upon in previous connections.

A prevalent error is to regard the alternatives in choice as a conflict of independent and distinct forces struggling for supremacy over the will as a something objectively distinct from themselves. Whereas, as a matter of fact, they have no power of themselves, but are what they are as our diversely appointed conceptions struggling toward that ultimate form which is reached in volition, will, choice, personal preference, as it is variously phrased. It is to be remembered that we have, here, a personal agent who conceives the alternatives, walking with such motives, purposes, desires, etc., as he can prefer and make his own, and finally acting upon that select conception which explodes in fulfilled desire, or responsible choice, as I have so often explained.

XII

In this section, I propose to offer some speculations upon the problem of ancestral heredity, and its power to enfold our future in a germ cell, which, it is alleged, predetermines choice.

What, then, shall we say of such a power, stored up in a germ cell? Well, for my part, so long as it gives us an express individuality of our own, I would not have one bit of it expurgated, for my benefit. Let it severely alone, as long as it is not some blighting abnormality. For, speaking generally, and after allowing for all manner of differences, I am unable to see, how such a cell has any more power to cripple choice with predetermination than any ordinary sensation, climatic conditions, or wide vistas of mountain and valley, or even the cult of peoples with whom we live, etc., etc. There

is, to be sure, quite a wide diversity of effects produced by these diverse agencies, but the make-up
of individual choice is not robbed of one iota of its
prerogatives. Every exterior power has a distinct
office to perform, in respect of thought, but none
can disturb the right of choice, under normal conditions. Give each man the proper humanities of
the race, and you have race responsibility, normal
experiences, alternative choice, free determinations
and morals.

But I am not now committed to the task of saying any more on that aspect of the subject. The
point to be investigated is the relation of the
present self and its present powers to the predeter-
minant powers of the germ cell.

And here let me say, that any amount or quality
of power packed away in a germ cell, that goes
only to the birth, being, and capabilities of the
individual, is simply an ordinance of God, in accordance with which such an individual must walk, in
order to be free and without which a free choice
would be a failure. And this is as far as any germ
cell can go. It gives us an individual being, and
remits us to an individual choice; that is all.

But then, says an objector, this your germ cell,
walking so innocently before your sweet individuality, is charged with the virus of innumerable
other germ cells, coming down from the remote
past, and piling upon you a huge mass of predeter-
mining influences which you cannot away with.

Very correct, and cheerfully conceded is all this
talk about one's ancestors; and you must not sup-

pose that we could wish to part company from them. The man's individuality and responsibility, — his power of thought and choice, for all that, is left intact. And no amount and no strength of an ancestral germ cell can determine anything for him contrary to a present act of thought, or choice. The power of thought never lets up in the presence of any genetic force, so long as the man's proper humanities and individuality are not evicted.

XIII

I conclude with some detached observations bearing upon the problems remarked upon in the immediately preceding sections. Choice is determined by motives, qualitatively appointed for going upon a final act. But, strictly speaking, a motive is an end or purpose conceived in order to choice. And, therefore, choice implies a searching, preparatory study of all the problems which bear upon our personal responsibility for what we are about to do, as well as also final consent and conation. Hence, the problem of volition must forever rest upon the view we can take of our personal well-being and responsibility; a careful allowance being made for exterior potencies, present or antecedent, whose presence and power we may by no means ignore.

We are not omniscient, but, though finite, we hold ourselves responsible for what we do, often blundering on the way to our objective purpose. Still, if we are really doing our best to reach some conclusion upon which we may be free to act by right of the conceptive power of our own thoughts, that is to say, by the power of choice or a prevailing reason, we have not striven in vain. We are simply doing our best, under our finite conditions and limitations and in our various callings, to bring our best thought and experience to bear upon the problems of life, and in pursuance of those loftier ambitions which are denied to orders of intelligence where thought and animal impulse are more at one.

The process is an act of attention, deliberation, and comparison, whereby a conception of alternatives and a judgment on their contrasting pretensions clears the way to a final eligible conception which we call our choice.

And having thus discovered a conception adequate to the demands of choice and personal responsibility, we set this conception forward upon our contemplated work; for thought not only illumines our path, but directs, decides, and completes our purposed tasks.

Finally, analyze thought as we may, there is still left over a vast residuum of ever present conditions, such as sensations, dispositions, mental, moral, and physical endowments, heredity, environment, etc., etc., whose office, as heretofore explained, is to give thought the competency and opportunity to conceive a line of action for itself within the limitations fixed by said conditions. And as thus limited, its essential prerogatives, as a rational, volitional, and responsible cause, are no more infringed upon than those of matter and even God (be they what they may) are infringed upon by conditions and limitations which prescribe and qualify a mode of being and activity for them. For, beyond the special nature, or strictly inner life of anything, there is an infinite number of other entities, with diversely qualified functions and powers, whose presence and rôle of action thought can by no means overlook, but which, for their part, can by no means do, or undo, what is the office of thought to do.

Moreover, though thought must depend upon its conditions, surroundings, etc., these can never explain choice, whatever may be their office. For thought has a character and competency, peculiar to itself; even as the thronging potencies which confront it on every side have what is individual to themselves. But to say that either the one or the other can step beyond his natural province, and, under the usual conditions of action and interaction, supplant or suppress the distinctive individuality of the other, is not only unphilosophical and unpsychological, but utterly recalcitrant to any scheme of reason which would provide for, and conserve, the action and interaction of the two.

CHAPTER XXI

Ourself or Soul

We have life and thought compacted together, in a variety of ways, by the bond of personal interest in all we do, securing thus a casting vote without schism among the parts. We never see life as an undifferentiated integer. It is ever a memberment of parts coöperating as contributory factors in subordination to a central whole. I refer to that power which, whilst securing a regulated concert of action among the parts, perfectly conserves their diverse functions. Life is memberment, plus a central authority which is single, personal, and supreme over all the parts. It has no expression, no meaning, no existence even, — except as thus rendered.

I

It is objected, however, that there is no *proof* of this unit of power within experience and observation. "How know we it? All we know is sensations," etc. On the other hand, I contend that the proof is through experience and observation; that all our experiences, even that of a sensation, are discursive achievements depending on some power of mind to judge and avouch what we observe.

A sensation is known, and can be known, only by the marks that accredit it. All knowledge founds on the same power, namely, that which achieves the idea of a sensation, emotion, relation, or anything else, and discriminates one idea or object from another. It comes of the heaven-born ability to judge and distinguish by traits, or marks which identify objects of knowledge. In other language, we *infer* life, cause, soul, etc., even as, from a perturbation in the sensorium, we conclude that it is a sensation, and not a cognition,— a something which is not an act of the power that undertakes to know it. Indeed, we verify everything, just as we prove the existence of our neighbors, by the unanswerable logic of their footprints, or other marks of life and thought.

Remarking now, more particularly, upon the evidences for ourself or soul, I note that the inference is not locally remote, like many we draw. An immediate judgment affirms the immediate cause of our subjective acts; as also the *kind* of causes is likewise determined by an immediate appraisement of the character of the conceptions transpiring under the direct gaze of consciousness: just as, when our attention is directed to acts of right and wrong, we are remarking their contrasting values, affirming and appraising, at one and the same time, and equally, acts and their kind or character,— of course somewhat vaguely, but still intelligently, upon our first intercourse with such facts. And similarly, whenever we are regarding the acts of a subjective cause, we are affirming ourselves as their conscious cause.

For consciousness implies a conscious actor,

solely because, in conscious acting, we are the conscious actor; the judgment embracing and affirming simultaneously one as much as the other.

Here I may explain that what we are affirming is an action and an actor given in a concrete presentation, the judgment avouching both simultaneously and directly, and therefore the affirmation of both is instantaneous, for you cannot affirm an action severed from an actor. And this is emphatically true of conscious thinking, the affirmation of which involves the coëtaneous affirmation of a conscious thinker or soul.

But for that matter, how could one affirm anything without, then and there, affirming himself as the affirmer. Besides, there can be no difference in affirming an act of mind and affirming mind as an actor.

The reader need not be reminded that the discursive acts just mentioned are, for the most part, but the beginnings of thought. But though it proceeds from a present, conscious, mental act, seen (at first) in the concrete as an indivisible part, to the actor seen as its counterpart, it advances from the attributes immediately affirmed to the remoter things which manifest them, and from things to a coördination of their statics and dynamics, reaching finally a clear conception of the personal and moral problems suggested by such fruitful discoveries.

II

And so, we conceive ourselves to be what our acts indicate,—nothing beyond. I am aware of a

prevalent illusion which bids us find something
distinct from the mind and its phenomenal manifestations; a something outside of what we know of
the mind as a self-conscious activity; a *substratum*
or essence, in which the mind, and its powers,
inhere. But this is a plunge into an abyss utterly
void of any tangible support. I know nothing, and
can say nothing, of such an essence. All I can
affirm is some really existing thing, such as mind
or matter; and I can know it only by what it is
and does.

As an activity, mind must work as it knows. It
cannot grapple with its work without the power of
some thought enlisted in its performance. But the
soul cannot be said to be present as a free cause, or
personal and responsible unit of action, until we
have the aims which come of an intelligent development of our discursive possibilities. It must,
once for all, be born. We must have command of
all our cognitive resources. Neither the will, nor
any act for which we are responsible, can come
sauntering into notice, unbidden of the soul. And,
though we may rightly regard the will, emotions,
desires, etc., as indispensable forces, at our service,
yet the real efficiency is with the rational unit, or
responsible soul. Forasmuch, then, as these are
our instrumental forces, we ourself, as differentiated by organs, capacities, etc., determine our conduct through them. Upon us is laid the burden of
conceptive power,— not upon them,— and we alone
are responsible for the manner in which that power
is employed.

You remark that the moral unit does not take the character of a pronounced, personal cause, until it has carefully cleared the way to a mature responsibility for its acts.   It has to await the occasion of its discovery and appreciation of moral distinctions and needs, ere it can act on them.   In order to the empire of mind and morals, it must have acquired the ideas of right and wrong, good and bad, mine and thine, duty, obligation, etc., upon which to found an adequate conception of itself as a power, single, personal, and responsible. Otherwise how could the variant hopes and fears, joys and sorrows, aims, anxieties, and bothers of life, be combined, and not antagonized, in conduct? Moreover, though we might acquire all knowledge, yet, if we could not employ it as an innovating, reconstructive power for our own good or bad, we could never build up acts for which we are individually and personally responsible, and so could not be ourself.

III

The will in particular, as tested by these considerations, is simply the force of our final conception, or if you prefer, the force of our final reason or judgment.   For, what one does by any of his members, he does himself.   If he is only meditative, he does that work; if purposing, that work; if acting or willing, that work.

It seems plain, therefore, that, when we affirm ourself, or ego, or soul, or person, as the doer of an act, we are affirming a unit of power that carries the force of our convictions into what we do. Now the will, viewed as our executive power, is but ourself going along with our most urgent reasons. For we cannot be personally responsible for either will or reasons, emotions or desires, or anything mental or moral, which undertakes to do duty as an *outside* factor. And so, it all comes to this, that the man himself, as rational and responsible, acquires and wields a power he has acquired in acquiring his informations. And, therefore, have we a personal power which takes character from the grade of our mental and moral distinctions; and we advance in power, *pari passu* with every advance in knowledge.

IV

Holding these views, I venture a version of what transpires in an act of free determination in accordance with my theory of discovering power as we discover knowledge.

My first remark is that there is no call for any of our psychical members to be free. Are any of them responsible? As previously suggested, motives or reasons, and the will, are not to be regarded as competing for supremacy in acts of choice. Man's motives, even emotions, desires, and the will, are his own by reason of the acts of exploration and discovery which made them his, just as his will is his own rational impulse, because born with and part of the informations he acquires.

There is no segregated action of motives upon the will, much less can the will be disjoined from motives or informations and left to work up for

T

itself an executive power, personal and voluntary. Man is a sole energy in all he does, acquiring, and having full command of, every information whose final stringency is utilized in the crisis of responsible performance. A sane man cannot do anything without a sufficiently strong reason for what he does.

The story is the same in whatever way we may handle the facts before us. The soul is the rational centre for both thought and act. The organs and capacities are our own. Thought gives power. But the doing of anything, in any way, does not alter the essential fact that we do it ourself, on deliberation and responsible choice. For, whenever we act, we unite, adjust, and direct our every spiritual member to secure those conjoint results known as our deeds or works. We do it all.

Our personal power is as distinctly seen in one act as in another; in the most ordinary, as in the most complicated act of reasoning; in what is simply tentative and preliminary, as in that last, grim *nisus*, or effort, which delivers the works of our hands. For whilst our members have no action of their own, certainly none exterior to, and causative of, the unitary power which combines and controls their action, they act ever in concert and subordination, as social factors under charge of the above unitary power.

You see that we are regarding our spiritual organism as differentiated by a variety of social members under the control of a responsible factor which acts with undivided sovereignty in the sphere of thought and deed, and is therefore responsible for both.

Now, the logic of the situation would be wholly changed, if the parts could act independently. On that supposition, we should have thought without *our* thinking; will, purpose, choice, conduct, character, etc., without our being in either one or the other. Besides, if we regard our psychical members as acting independently of each other, we should invoke another batch of absurdities, such as perception, without conception, and *vice versa;* or information, without desire or emotion; or choice, without any logical elaboration, òr ultimating reason of *our own;* and so on, to the end.

The fact of the unitary power of the mind stands firm against all criticism. It is seen that neither severalty nor schism is allowed among the psychical members. Each yields a distinct, but regulated, social service to the federal head. And the latter, in turn, enforces a guarded responsibility by a thoughtful employment of the subordinate instrumentalities.

A supreme ruler, we are not dependent on the will, or any subservient member, for any help *exterior* to our authority. An autocrat, with an individuality and domestic economy of our own, we act on judgment and personal responsibility; never permitting our subordinates to step out of the line of subservience to our behests and set up superserviceable actions of their own, lest we invite the instant subversion of our discursive individuality.

V

My debate will conclude with a synopsis of preceding views.

Our soul is a unit of functions, each of which contributes a scheme of service called forth at the command of the former, and without a trace of extraneous, or otherwise intrusive, action on their part. For, whatever be their rôle of action, it is but the action of the soul, when employed in rational work.

Neither the will, nor motives or reasons, nor emotions and desires, can perform the office of a supreme, personal functionary. Our freedom cannot recognize the action of factors partitively pushing their way into independent results.

We must act as *persons*, personally responsible for our acts. Our psychical forces are but constituent elements of a discursive energy which undertakes to know, and then acts as it knows. What we call the will, for example, is but the force of our decisive thought, and, therefore, a power of our own.

Grant me thought, and I have its power or urgency, and this same urgency is my personal power or will, going into all I do. Our thought, with its executive power,—called emotion or desire, in reference to the instructed soul or *person;* called the will, when referring more directly to our executive, or ultimating *power*,—is, therefore, our sole efficiency in responsible conduct.

CHAPTER XXII

REVIEW OF THE ARGUMENT

THOUGHT affirms an object and points out some of its attributes, namely, some of its statics and dynamics, and their phenomenal relations, individual or social. And, therefore, it affirms some real things, — not phantoms, — and not merely matter, but the realities of its own activities as well.

It is powerless to affirm a nonentity; for the latter is neither reality nor attributes. Nor can it affirm chaos; for that has no principle of being or action, and so neither substance nor attributes, and, therefore also, no points of connection or relation with either thought or things.

I

But in virtue of its contact with its sensor organs, mind becomes conscious of a non-conscious excitation in the sensorium. Now it is this excitation, or sensation, that the mind first feels in vague, unripe cognition, and afterward *perceives* in clearer cognition; and this is all it does perceive in sensible perception. The sensation is immediately presented to the mind, and the latter immediately perceives it; achieving thus the naked idea of a non-conscious energy acting on itself. For I take

perception to be the readiest cognition of something whose features, or detailed individual attributes, have not then been, or else need not be,
carefully abstracted and accredited, on reflection
and logical elaboration. In fact, at the stage of
perception, the soul does not feel committed to the
task of affirming or denying any details, with particular care. It simply beholds a something which
is not itself, and which it can so affirm. But, as
soon·as it can detach and study characteristic features, it is on the point of mediating and correlating
remoter and broader ideas, by means of conception
and logic.

Perceptive knowledge is relatively limited, the
mind not having certified anything beyond a concrete impression in the sensorium, exterior to itself,
and so not having any rational conceptions; and
since it has not attained to a view of objects, as
founded on laws, forms, changes, features, and the
unalterable relationships which bind each of them,
as a part of knowledge to the whole which includes
the assemblage of characteristic features,— since
it has not done this, it does not have such a knowledge of itself and other things, as will enable it to
elicit a conception of its own wants, and to act
accordingly.

On the contrary, the office of conception is to
ponder the ideas reached by perception, compare
notes with the attributes of objects and elicit their
logical affiliations. It begins an active exploration
of such objects as it perceives, fixing attention on,
say, some particular kind of energy and tracing it

back to some outer or inner potency, or else contrasting one attribute with another, or with others,
— or with ideas and emotions; or else discriminating it as voluntary from a non-voluntary activity,
and so on, until it has mastered the facts and
principles upon which it can act as a responsible
person.   But I may not go into further details in
this place.

II

Man is a personal power, taking a personal
interest in all that transpires within the purview
of his thoughts.   His feelings are enlisted.   He is
now a *person*.

Hence arise various emotions, answering to the
diverse character of his informations.   He may
have attained to æsthetic and moral conceptions.
If so, his personal interest will be manifested by
emotions which will express their character and
power.   For one must have acquired the ideas of
the true, the beautiful, the sublime, — the good and
bad, right and wrong, — ere the attaching interest
can report itself emotionally.

And he is the more impressively emotioned,
because, being human, he comes to know that he
has secured these personal motors through the
watchful interest he takes in constructing a life
of rational impulsions and satisfactions.

Remark distinctly that, when our emotions found
on conceptions of moral good and evil, any power
they may have over conduct is perfectly consistent
with our personal freedom, and this for the plain

reason that all our higher emotions are called forth by some fact, sought out of the mind, which determines their being and mission.

"The hidden man of the heart" is, in fact, never hidden from the power of mind. We may go off into wild ways when led by vile emotions. This is part of the dowery of freedom. But it does not change the dependence of emotion on thought. The latter may be as wild as the dependent emotions, and still direct them. Whenever we come to ourselves, like the prodigal son, we have simply returned to a previous condition of mind and morals wherein we could think differently and determine our emotions accordingly. We may review and amend our ways, on occasion of a sufficient experience of the penalties inflicted for moral dereliction. For when one's views change, his emotions change with them.

III

In foregoing discussions it was shown that, by cultivating his powers, man walks as a differentiated and conscious integer, having power to liberate an executive energy which goes into his work or conduct. I would now retouch this discussion, for reasons of clearer perceptive — if indeed our freedom is not an illusion.

Be that as it may, it does not consist in any efficiency separate from that of thought. It is not to be found in the will, viewed as an independent, self-acting, free cause. But it is in the ego, or responsible soul, freely acquiring knowledge, and freely using its power in matters of choice and responsible determinations.

But, as a striking feature in the conception and choice of work is the display of sufficient power to do the work, philosophers seem agreed to call that power the will in distinction from other mental powers,— many holding that it steps in at the opportune moment, and somehow or other, makes us free by an impulse of its own, even in the presence of our decisive reasons.

To all which the facts elicited in past discussions give ample denial. There is no such thing as the will acting upon or for the man, or upon or for his reasons, and imparting to either, or both, a voluntary efficiency not already theirs. The man himself, as rational, controls himself by the power of his reasons, effectuating choice by the conscious employment of the power of his ideas in all he does. The man thinks, and wills, as he thinks. For doing at will, or by the will, is doing as one thinks or opines; accomplishing in act or deed that, for the doing of which, his informations have furnished him the requisite power,— the result being that, in all he does, man is impelled by his strongest reason, and can never, at all, act without it.

Another point previously made may be adverted to in this connection. It is to this effect, that, as man cannot perform a work by simply getting ready for it, he must find some way of giving finality to his opinions, or reasons. An opinion whose force is smuggled out of the way in the crisis of performance, does not possess the required efficiency. Besides, it must have a purposed, practical stringency, if the thinker is to be charged with personal responsibility for his act.

An inexorable code of reason requires us to excogitate some power of thought which will do our work, and show us when to do it, in order to our having any intelligent command of the reasons why we should be charged with doing it. For, if we do a work by conceptive power, we know it is ours by a power of our own.

I confess to some anxiety to give these distinctions in clearest outline. I am holding to the view that man is competently equipped for acquiring knowledge, and making use of its power, in his acts. In virtue of the fact that he is a unit of body and mind, he has command of the resources of both. And, in virtue of his preëminent capacity for discursion, and in behalf of the susceptibilities which he cultivates and makes use of, he advances upon the worlds of mind and matter, and wins from them a wide range of unwonted transformations, due solely to the force and dignity of his cognitions. In other words, he is an innovator,—a setter-up of a strange power, affronting and remodelling the unchanging use and wont prevailing in the world of material causes and sequences. And he does it all by employing a power which is born with his thoughts. The force of his thoughts, or reasons, is his sole efficient in what he does.

IV

Turning now, for a moment, to a more articulate treatment of the function of reasons, informations, etc., we are to regard them as man's all-sufficient resources in the work of his hand; finalizing his thoughts, in finalizing his work. And, whatever impelling force they may have is his own; the fact of his achieving and employing them constituting him a free agent, and personally responsible for his acts. He himself is ever in, and with them, either as a discursive presence remarking their special characters, and discriminating their social affiliations, or else actively choosing them, in some final procedure.

Let me hope that the following incident may serve to make this securely plain: I see one fording a river on horseback. He is holding up his feet. But now, why hold them up? The reason is plain. He is moved by reasons, or informations, which will have it, that it is for his good. But, it is so that his feet still tip the water, and, thereupon, he elevates them still higher. The motive here is likewise manifest. He is informed of the unpleasant results which follow such watery indiscretions, and would now protect himself from their recurrence. So, from every point of view, we see that man's actions come at the call of his reasons, and he always acts as they urge him, walking very literally "in all their commandments and ordinances," without the trace of a single deviation.

And yet, man is a free agent, and cannot be free

in any other way.   For, as so often explained, his
informations are his own powers, made his own by
right of discovery and conquest, and so are not
made over to him by any power *ab extra*.   And,
therefore, if they do determine his will, or acts, or
conduct, it is his own thought that does it.   He
has been at pains to acquire, and now puts forth
the power, thus acquired, to go upon his work, and
do it, and so, he, alone, is responsible.   No one
can take thought of the attributes and potencies of
things of himself and things not himself, in his
stead, and so, no one can do for him what is personal and responsible in his judgments of choice
and action.   And if he thinks he has a will, and
should employ it as a subservient instrumentality
for giving effect to his reasons, he would still
be employing the power of his informations and
giving them wonted sanction in conduct.

A pertinent example will explain all this.   A
certain man has an opinion which habitually controls his conduct.   Suppose, now, that a neighbor
should attempt to give him one that he could not
make his own, and so control his conduct differently.   Would he not literally talk out the psychological facts speaking in his soul, if he should
object: "This thing you propose, will never do.
It would contravene my freedom, and make me
your slave.   If you give me your opinions, and
deny me mine, — why, sir, I am a mere machine.
I lose myself and personal responsibility besides,
when I lose my own opinions.   You think to give
me your opinions, and make them mine, but if I

cannot have my own, and give them full play and power, in the determination of my own conduct, you fracture that organic oneness of soul, by which it is possible for me alone to determine my conduct and responsibility in their untrammelled correlations.   I cannot afford to vacate my freedom and personal identity at one and the same time.   I dance to my own piping in the affairs of thought and conduct.   My opinion is mine; your opinion is yours, and away with it."

This language wears the air of an indignant challenge, and rightly, because it is a defence of personal right and competency.   You observe that the speaker plants his freedom on his own opinions. He has no quarrel with that.   But he protests vigorously against its being founded on opinions not his own.   He must have his own way of solving the problems of life, and so hold himself, and not his neighbor, responsible for his conduct. And, therefore again, I conclude that a man stands as his thoughts stand, acting only as he is informed and impelled by them, and that, whatever he may do, and with whatever instrumentality, — be it emotion, desire, or will, or even his physical members, so far as he can command their service, — the sole and indispensable efficiency resorted to in consummating his voluntary and responsible endeavors is the force of his reasons, or convictions.

One or another of us has seen or read of something like the following: A great general matures his plans, marshals his forces, and tramples upon the columns of his enemy.   A battle is fought and won.   He had to rely on the prompt service of powder and ball as instrumentalities to be availed of in aid of his plans.   But in accounting for his bloody laurels, it would amaze us to hear one say: "The powder and ball achieved the victory."   That would be (to use, perhaps, a familiar illustration) much like accounting for the production of some great picture, not by the æsthetic and constructive appreciations of the painter, but by the want of thought in the pigments.

Victory will forever perch upon the banner of the general whose power of thought conceives, and executes, such efficient combinations as a disciplined and faithful soldiery are competent to carry out in practice.   Powder and ball and paint are but matter, fundamentally remodelled of thought for carrying special concepts forward into conceived results.   Result is victory.

A thought, once born, halts not short of some achievement.   And once born, it is henceforth our personal and responsible energy.   It is renewed and reformed with every process of discursion.   It is immortal.

V

As constituting a feature of my discussions, I submit a few words upon the part played by the appetites, as native propensities, in relation to that of thought.   As native forces they lend support to our animal and vital economy, preparing the way for the conquests of discursion.   And, so

far as they are not tempered by the latter, their
action is wholly involuntary. And yet, in time,
they become so habitually under the latter's charge,
that they make only such demands as bespeak its
responsible supervision and sanction. That is to
say, they depend on thought for a *rational* instigation.

Allowing, then, for what is voluntary and involuntary in our nature, we may see how the
continuity of reason is kept up; in part, by the
persistent importunity of our animal and vital,
and, in part, by our mental and moral needs.
And in this we have a way appointed, not only
for life, but for rational work, as well. Indeed,
thought could never, at all, enter upon its destined
work without these unthinking, sensorial perturbations. Nor could it ever have a conception beyond
them, save when, on occasion of their emergence,
or that of similar sensations, it essayed the discovery of its own powers. But let an impulse be
simply vital or animal, or mental or moral, or
mixed, and whether the ego be ready or getting
ready, the ideas on which we act are of our own
procurement, and accomplish the work of our
choice, or prevailing reason.

VI

Similar remarks apply to emotions and desires.
In acts of choice, for instance, what are they but
the personal and voluntary phase of some final
thought which overbalances some alternative one?
For, as previously intimated, though neither alter-

native has any power of competition except what thought imparts, yet, as intelligent impulsions, they occupy the position of release from, or advance upon, our blind impulsions. Further remarks are reserved for the chapter on the Will.

VII

Similar observations obtain in the treatment of dispositions. In a former chapter I have shown how they subserve our rational ends and work. And here again, I repeat that we still act, as we are informed.

Ponder carefully the following incident: I once consulted a lawyer about some land I had purchased, the title to which some other party had subsequently disputed. He asked me if I had made any promises of payment to the creditor, after the title had become clouded. I replied, "Certainly, if such a question had ever been propounded to me."

Now, for the drift of this incident. 1. It discloses an affirmed identity of person, at two different periods separated by years. 2. It asserts the power of my dispositions (here character) over my conduct; otherwise I had not affirmed that I must have promised payment. 3. It affirms that the dispositions or character are an ever-present power for which I am responsible, as a conscious, continuous, determinant of my actions, past or present.

And this is plainly what is meant by one's dispositions affecting one's conduct. Speaking so confidently of what I would have said, I must have known my moral character as a power over my conduct. It is to be understood, however, that whatever power there may be in dispositions or character, has been built up by dint of the informations, that so form and transform it, that it is made ours in contradistinction from another's. And so, here too, we are beholden to reasons, ideas, informations, etc., for conceiving and shaping character; giving us rational power and egoistical responsibility.

But I call up another example to illustrate and support my contention. We take kindly to a child, let us say, because we love it. Now, it is apparent that, whatever may be the content of this sentiment it is mine, and, therefore, if moved to do the child a kindness, some motive of tenderness would impel me. But what put it into my soul, and held it there so stubbornly that I could so confidently and correctly claim it to be *mine?* The answer is that the whole past of my life has been one unending quest for informations, — some tender, gentle, affectionate, some æsthetic, some softly beautiful, some flower-like and bright,— and I discovered and fixed the sentiment forever in my soul.

And I may say that you may take any moment of the past, be it away back at the beginning, and if it be a question how I came by either motives or personal character, there can be but one answer: Every factor that dares to control, or has controlled me, I made my own by the quality and power of my own thoughts, unless, perchance, I lost my personal powers and identity in the meantime.

I notice that my remarks are becoming, more and

U

more, egoistical if not egotistical. But then, there are reasons for this, too. For I would have it understood that, in rational determinations, we have to deal with the person, or ego, and in this way have every act egoistical or personal, *i.e.*, gone upon for reasons of personal effort and responsibility.

VIII

It may, however, still be objected that whatever acts on the ego, must necessitate thought to that extent. Now, I do not controvert that view, when properly explicated. But it is misleading, in that it does not give a fair view of the prerogatives of thought. I admit that it takes many things to put a free cause in place for entering upon its discursive functions. And no one can object to the binding force of the enabling laws which support, and conserve, the rational procedures, on which we are free to think and act. But, what is all this pre-arrangement for the necessary action of exterior things, upon us, but the complement of prerequisites furnished of God, in order to the incoming of our voluntary competencies? And why should not thought be informed of the presence and power of neighboring, and co-active, entities? What forbids our having neighbors on such terms as will allow our being so conversant with them and their ways, that we may be profited by as much as we can discover of them and their ways? Certainly, it is from these thronging potencies, — thought's outside objects, — that we discover the very informations which fit us for dealing with them efficiently, in consummating all our voluntary undertakings.

Indeed, if we are ever to have discursive liberty in acts, it is all in the power of thought to gain such knowledge of neighboring potencies,—be they native endowments or what not,—as will enable us to square our conduct by what we know of them. It is a question of two potencies, one discursive, the other material, naturalistic, or else animal. The former must know the powers of the latter, as well as those of itself, in order to the performance of acts in accordance with what it knows of both.

CHAPTER XXIII

A Self-acting Will

Some philosophers deny to reason the power to determine the will, or acts; seeking man's freedom in a self-acting will, so called. A brief examination will disclose the curious psychological perversions of this theory.

However, if we are free through the self-action of the will, it may be of some interest to see how such action makes us free, and to connect (if we can) the logical conclusions with that freedom. I protest, though, that I regard such a will as a nondescript factor with which I have no acquaintance, — its apostles reporting its features in vaguest verbiage. It is to be hoped, however, that we can presently see how this fantastic self-action of the will can be got to work in the tackle of truth.

1. I remark that if there is really no need of a will, taken as something distinct from the inherent force of our reasons, then, why should we improvise this additional factor, which claims to be not only distinct from the force of our thoughts, but self-acting? There must be some very incoherent thinking on the part of one who, in constructing a theory to relieve us of the efficiency and sufficiency of motives, clutters it up with such incongruous and unphilosophical padding.

2. As to the fundamental facts of volition, my position is now perhaps so well known, that I recur to it only as a reminder in passing. I repeat that, if we would do anything, we must have a conception of the thing to be done, and then follow it up by a decisive reason for doing it; and we do it by the power which is born with our decisive reason. This seems explicit, to a finish.

However, it is allowable to suppose that there may be another force standing outside of this final and decisive reason. But even then, it could not be said to be self-acting, if it be found habitually to conform to the appreciations of the former. So then, if the same potency that conceives and concludes to do things, *in posse*, instantaneously and actually does them, there is no more necessity for excogitating an independent and self-acting will than for an independent and self-acting memory, judgment, imagination, or divers other elaborative processes. Such facts as these proclaim the man himself, or say, in a phrase, the power of his thought, and nothing else, to be the sole energy resorted to in conception and act.

The power of some reason determines all he does — a power which is not withdrawn in the presence of a self-acting will, if there should be any such. But for that matter, even if such a will should attempt to block the way of an energy so resistless as a decisive reason, the shock of the conflict would amount to zero, the power of reason forever exacting a rigorous conformity to its behests.

3. A self-acting will cannot achieve our free-

dom. The impossible feat would make us slaves to a neighboring factor, playing the rôle of an officious intermeddler. Psychology is of stubborn facts, not baseless surmises, otherwise we can affirm, or deny, as we list, and get only rubbish for our pains. "It is in facts that we must seek general principles, and these must always accord with the facts," says Aristotle.

I delay to ponder this teaching, for a moment, in connection with the facts of our active and forceful intelligence, — as seen in the power of our informations. Founding on reasons, consciously our own, we have achievements, consciously our own; and if thus consciously our own, where can a self-acting will come in, — if at all? An interloper is a born outsider, without knowledge and without its power. Moreover, if we act as we think, nothing can divide our responsibility, for we are equally and impregnably conscious of having won such informations as fix the value of our own, and others', acts, and define the confines of the *meum* and *tuum* of each.

And therefore, let me insist that, if we are the cause of our acts through the force of our reasons, it cannot be denied that we are responsible for them; and that much being settled beyond controversy, the claims made for the non-determination of conduct by motives or reasons must fall to the ground.

So, too, we can have no need to soften down, or else avoid, the force of our sinful motives, lest we question an ordinance of God by which they act efficiently for our good or bad, in defiance of the evasive self-sufficiency of a self-acting will. The urgency for some clever way of relieving God of responsibility for sin is not so apparent just here, seeing we are free through a conscious achievement of informations, consciously ours, and for which we are, therefore, consciously responsible.

4. But other anomalies coming in, almost unannounced, may explain this pet scheme of a self-acting will. Though the will is put forward as a self-acting energy, I am inclined to opine that it is, nevertheless, not so. For, inasmuch as it is confessedly our will, its action must be ours also; and if ours, what becomes of the theory of self-action?

5. It must be independent, in some way or other. But if so, — how?

6. It cannot be both independent and dependent. And yet, it is both. For, whereas they dogmatically asseverate its self-action, they nevertheless argue that this self-action must, in some way, be man's; and if so, it is a dependent energy.

7. If it is either singly, then the other is a myth. But query, which of the two is non-mythical?

8. If you destroy a self-acting will, the theory falls to pieces, and nobody is hurt. For man may yet be free through the constructive might of his intellections.

Contrariwise, if you destroy our will as our own conscious energy going into acts of conduct and choice, then you are in this position: You have destroyed that power in thoughts by which you have any choice or preference in acts, and have no power henceforth even to conceive how a self-acting will can make over to you a conscious achievement of your own.

We must have a will of our own for our own action. The theory for any action extraneous to the power of thought is untenable.

9. If the will is to be made self-acting, and so can act from its own centre, in order to free it from the power of motives or reasons, then the man himself is not free. For moral rectitude and wrong depend on right and wrong motives.

10. And furthermore, if it is self-acting, and so can act independently, whence comes the turpitude of our acts? Especially, how can man sin, when, though he may feel his sinful motives much as one feels a sensation, the power to employ them in conduct remains with a self-acting will, beyond his control?

11. Or, as a possible alternative, do motives, after all, really influence the will? But if so, what becomes of the surplus and extraneous factor of its self-action?

12. As man is free (let us concede) not through the efficiency of his thought, but in virtue of a self-acting will, it is in fact not he that is free, but really and only his self-acting will. And so, we have again the same old, redoubtable anomaly that, whilst he, for his part, has no power of thought for his determinations, the self-acting will, being, for its part, the real efficient in conduct, alone is the author of sin, and the man himself is guiltless.

But, if such a will can exploit this unconditioned fencing, then we have, on the one hand, man with a moral spontaneity, fitted for choice, and open to sin, but powerless for its commission, — because he cannot determine his way either to or from it. And so, on the other hand, we have God creating a being who can have sinful desires and cherish them, too (which is sin); and the man himself, — sinful though he be, — improvising an irresponsible factor of self-action to relieve his Creator, at the expense of his own freedom; and worse, the creature making himself and his Creator equally ridiculous by a theory which, besides being a failure, belittles and besmirches both.

13. As a self-acting will determines actions for itself (lest otherwise motives might determine man's actions), then, however much it may be acquainted with sin, it is nevertheless irresponsible. Divorcing itself from motives, it is in the condition of an idiot who knows of none to be divorced from.

14. I may mention another curious consequence resulting from this mistaken analysis of the facts of volition. Inasmuch as by this theory (see previous paragraphs) a man's reasons cannot determine his acts, he cannot, for that reason, be held responsible for them. Still, as they are determined by his vicar (the supposed self-acting will), notwithstanding the contradiction which is a perquisite of its self-action, he may yet be regarded as the real and responsible doer of them. For, what a man does by his vicar, he does *himself* (though, if the vicar act for himself, how can another lay claim to

his acts ?). However, inasmuch as man thinks he is free, there remains the possibility that his vicar has some way of commending to him the freedom and responsibility due to a competent thinker. Now let us think that he succeeds in this. Then, we have the man free by the self-action of his will, and all he has to do is to fold his arms and wait, until his vicar has made his freedom over to him, on condition, however, that it should in no case *cause* him to accept it, neither permit his *motives* to do so.

15. Here another formidable puzzle obtrudes itself : I am free to admit that, inasmuch as non-determinists are not over-careful in their language, it may after all be claimed that a self-acting will is man's, and that, therefore, whilst the Creator is exculpated from sin (seeing that, by the present supposition, it must rest with the voluntary act of the man who has such a will) it does not necessarily relieve the latter, now that he is furnished with such a will, at his command, if indeed he can command such a will. Now, we have here a self-acting will put forward to relieve God of responsibility for man's sinful thoughts and deeds. But you remember that such a will is placed outside and independent of motives, expressly to give it a self-sufficiency relieved of their power. (I have already mooted this point in other connections.)

But I wish now to see how this newer figment fits in with the known facts of thought and volition or choice. Granting such a will to be man's, it is to be remembered that non-determinists have it self-active, for the reason that neither the force of one's reasons nor that of anything else, save such a will, should determine our conduct. Bearing this in mind, I am tempted to propound the question: If such a will is so fledged with the self-sufficiency of self-action as to be independent of God as a causal efficient, in its own acts, and in this way exonerate Him from responsibility for the sins of Adam and his posterity, would it not, in like manner and for like reasons, also discharge any man with such a will from the guilt of sin? The logic is inexorable. If it exculpates one, it exculpates the other. Any kind of self-action devised expressly to traverse cause, and so have the Creator eliminated as, in any way, a responsible factor for what we see of sin, equally traverses the causal efficiency of our reasons, and with like result.

Such lavish blundering may be a trifle picturesque, but not very instructive.

The determinist handles these points in accordance with the known facts of volition and choice. He has an abiding faith in the power and office of his reasons. He argues: If the man himself does his acts, by the inherent force of his reasons — in other phrase, if he is endowed with the capacity for achieving knowledge and acting upon it — in that case, the act is his own, and he alone is responsible. For he walks by the light of the prevailing reasons or motives which he affirms; and these identify him with his acts, as having consciously conceived, and, then, exercised, a power to do them;

and therefore has he made himself consciously and personally responsible for the exercise of that power, in all he does. He sees the act is his, by conception and execution, and therefore, also the guilt or innocence, if there be any. Of this there is not even the faintest shadow of doubt in him, — any more than he can doubt of his conceiving the prevailing reason on which he acted. He is open-minded and trustful. He is not to be found poking about with a candle in hand, in order to discover how God could formulate a moral government of choice and personal responsibility for sin, and Himself be guiltless, ere he, for himself, could feel sure of the unspeakable responsibility which rests upon himself for the deliberate conception and choice of sin. His great concern is for himself and what is true of himself as a sinner, — true of the power of his sinful thoughts to fix the responsibility upon himself for his sinful acts. And here, he is above all things sure, beyond all doubt; sure of conceiving a power of thought for finalizing and actualizing choice; sure of his sin and the resulting personal responsibility for its commission.

CHAPTER XXIV

The Will

I

A DISCUSSION of the will is a discussion of ultimating reasons or opinions, or choice. Expounded distinctly, the will is the inborn force of our final or decisive reason. The explanation has been explicitly outlined in preceding pages, somewhat after the following manner: You have opinions of some kind, such that you are in the position of one who is about to take some final action. And these antecedent opinions prepare the way for your taking that final action or step. And now, when you actually take that step, you must also have an opinion, or reason, for that too. Suppose, now, that you are engaged in the very act of taking that step. What becomes of the opinion in the instant of action? Can you annihilate it *instanter*, and do the act without your reason, or reasons, — improvising an alien force, for the nonce? May be, you could not. But, even if you could, you would still have to conceive a reason for that too; and you would be exactly where you were before, — acting on your last reason.

II

So then, we are driven to the conclusion that thought, opinion, information, or reasons, is not an

insulated ideation posing listlessly as a mere subjective consciousness, but an activity going forward into act or conduct. And, if our opinions do
have this practical outlet, we must needs be adhering to them with a personal (here emotional and
desiderative) fervor, adequate to pass them over
into our acts; and if thus passed over, we have
gone upon an act of choice or preference, as I may
now explain more particularly.

An act of choice is an act of personal preference,
on mature reflection, let us think. For, here you
hold an opinion of personal preference so tensely
personal that you abide in, and side with it, it may
be, through all the successive stages and phases of
preparation and final consummation in act or deed.
The opinion is yours in conception and deed, —
" one and inseparable." You choose, or prefer, or
wed, all your acts.

But wherefore? Because an opinion of preference is but yourself, discursively working up to a
contemplated result. You have sought out your
final working opinion, and now you cannot play
fast and loose with it, and so recall the power you
are putting into it. In its various stages of progressive achievement, it had your support, and now
that you have come to an act of choice, you cannot
withdraw the same support. You have won the
power to act on your final thought, and a final
thought goes on to result, as remorselessly as an
iceberg.

To be sure, every opinion, in its earlier stages,
is held with a vigor, perhaps somewhat more cogni-

tive than actile, or finalizing. But then, as soon as it becomes final, it and its peculiar vigor become both conceptive and creative of a preferred work. I need not say that this vigor may be remarked even in the faintest perceptions, or the beginnings of thought. But then, as previously intimated, when it culminates in conduct or deed, the personal fervor becomes more intense, and so is given over to an actile or efficiently constructive effort.

Wherefore, I claim that, from every point of view, whatever may be the last phase of the thought we take for doing an act, we take the same in doing it. Or, to put it differently, we may say that what prepares us for doing an act reappears in the work we do as the power of our final discursion. It does our work.

And, to prevent misconception, let me say distinctly that this power of our last discursion, this personal fervor which is born in and with our decisive thoughts, is the sole, true cause of all our acts, passing over, as it does, into all we do, as our personal preference or choice, and giving us an act of volition or will. For an act of will is an act of volition, which, in turn, is nothing more or less than an act of personal preference, or choice, determined by a *prevailing* reason. So much to give my position explicitly.

III

I am fighting my way up to the mount whence we may see how a productive energy like thought, behaves itself when, upon reaching the crisis of performance, it would finish with its proposed task. And, I could wish to see more clearly, if possible, whether this power of thought which gives us preference or choice, is volition or will, or whatever else we may call the real cause of our acts.

As intimated above, similar considerations apply to questions of power in all knowledge, whether preparative or actile. For every information, be it perception or conception, or what not, has its peculiar power, which, on becoming final, issues in conduct as our voluntary cause. But this power of knowledge is the power of the person who acquires it. And, therefore, whenever we conceive an ultimating opinion or conviction, we have acquired a personal energy, called indifferently an intelligent impulsion or voluntary cause. Thought and its power is, then, the true cause of all we do, or can do.

It is, of course, gradually attempered by every increment of knowledge, every such increment telling (in the quality and vigor of the impulsion) of the degree of culture attained by the thinker, as may be seen from the following. Inform a mere child of the letters and civilization of Greece and Rome, and he would not be moved by the same impulses, either in kind or degree, as a cultivated scholar. In either case, however, the thing called opinion, or reason, or conviction, does not profess to be knowledge without at least a due *minimum* of mental and personal vehemence. It must have some *vim*, else it cannot live.

Now then, if the character of this vehemence is

measured by the amount and quality of mental and moral cultivation on hand at the moment of acting, it is evident that, by the *lex prioritatis*, every preceding opinion, whatever may be its peculiar contingent of power, is also to be measured by the extent of our, then, cultivation. And if this be so, then the impulse, which we call the will, is here again, as always, a constituent element of our thought or opinion, etc.; or a power in knowledge, without which no thought can pretend to maintain itself for an instant, whether preparatory or final.

And so we conclude, again, that the will is nothing, but the force of our final reason passing on to performance, and doing battle there as choice, or the personal fidelity of the thinker to his own prevailing reason.

Knowledge is *power, personal power,* and therefore the power of our thought is always on hand, and always in season.

The slightest consideration will confirm these views. A step backward, and we are with the child and its stormy passions and propensities, its immature conceptions and wildering emotions. It has yet to learn of the intelligent and more personal ardor inspired by wider vistas of knowledge.

It is mainly governed by a flush of impulses which proceed from a natural curiosity, or capacity, for knowledge, as seen in the many phases of childish wonder. For this infantile curiosity, be it understood, is to be explained as an original *datum,* not to knowledge, but to the thinking faculty

x

itself, — vesting it with discursive potentials and possibilities which become developed and actual in motives and conduct. And here, too, let me repeat, it must needs have emotions, such as fear, wonder, surprise, etc., corresponding with the broken lines of its juvenile conceptions.

And here, it will be readily seen that, since its mental powers can, then, be but slightly articulated, the emphasis of its thoughts, though present, is marked by the flux of indefinite and incomplete emotions, corresponding with the wavering articulation of its first ideas. However, these remarks are strictly applicable only to the initial stages of thought. For both native curiosity and infantile emotion are transformed into, or else remodelled by, rational potencies, as soon as these infantile efforts have stimulated the rational factor into an exercise of its conceptive and constructive functions.

And this suggests a further explanation. Whenever one achieves his first distinct idea, known to be such, he has rational power, — actile, desiderative, decisive, voluntary, — and at that very moment begins to be a *person*. For until he can have an idea, in clear distinct outline, he is but an animal, in the vegetative stage. Such an idea, thus distinctly outlined and affirmed, is then a personal power, because, in acquiring it, thus distinctly outlined, the child begins to rate himself as an individual energy distinct from objects not himself. But such an idea, be it ever so infantile, is at once information and infantile power, — the information and power of a *person*, — and therefore a personal conceit and power going into the infant's deeds and enouncing the force of personal convictions.

Thenceforward, mind and person grow up together, and the child is more and more governed by personal considerations; and now he essays to set up the signs of an intelligent interest, self-esteem, personal preference, and a judicious choice of such alternatives as found on these advanced appreciations. And as all these infantile considerations — now artless, now astute, but ever discriminating — grow and take on discursive power, the actile force of the child's ideas is undergoing a corresponding metamorphosis, and he begins to employ them in maturer acts of volition and choice. His will is born. He is a power unto himself.

IV

I now take advantage of these distinctions, in order to their application to acts of perception, more particularly.

We begin by perceiving, say, a disturbance in one of our sensor organs, called a sensation. Here we have achieved the idea of this disturbance. Now what is the power of this idea or information? Reflect a moment.

On its first appearance the child has no experience, and so may, for a season, have a weakness for the native (untrained) curiosity of the ante-rational period, and so realize action without any knowledge of those alternative considerations which modify its action in later years. If so, it will be more or less dazed by the craze of unbridled impulses which attract and distract its attention. But if the mind apprehend the sensation, and so make a distinction between it and its apprehension, or, if it see the disturbance to be one thing, and its conscious apprehension another, and thus bring this idea into relation with itself, — giving it a *meaning* and affirming its relation to itself as the party for thought, — it is so far forth enriched by the power of the ideas acquired. It is now a personal and voluntary power, capable of acting for itself within the confines of its limited experiences.

Turning, now, to informations sought out of conception and its wider sweep of vision, I note a corresponding accretion of power in ideas.

Here we found on a more varied experience, and regard everything with an interest more adultly personal and responsible. We have reached the point where we can act on conceptions, not alone of things external, but of what we can do with them in the interest of our self-conscious and calculated needs and prejudices.

But here conception, it were almost a folly to repeat, is reinforced and strengthened by an increase of personal interest, or egoism, developed in developing our own world of educated conceits and wants.

And here, again, we have reached the point where we can exercise a rational curiosity, admeasured by maturer thoughts. We have become a thoughtful, provident, watchful *person*, choosing, or else eschewing, everything out of a regard for the personal interests involved in building up ourselves.

But the force of every information thus acquired is the force of our personal and responsible distinctions. And if so, it becomes the motor force which irreversibly determines conduct. It is the Will.

So distinctly can the point be made out that each idea has a power peculiar to itself, and which goes into conduct as our conative energy! I have been careful to explain that the first, chronologically, may have but a *minimum* of the personal vehemence born with those which rest on a broader conception of our growing needs. Indeed, the conclusion we are driven to, on evidence, proceeds upon the indisputable fact that, whether we act upon a natural curiosity almost flagrantly juvenile, or from an intelligent view of the perilous responsibilities of a maturer choice, our informations gather power and quality from the degree of personal interest, — conservative, latitudinarian, or other, — developed in their acquisition. It seems, then, that every idea we achieve is just so much personal power, emotional or desiderative, at our service for consummating our purposes, — its vigor waxing more intensely personal, the more we uncover our personal wants, or educed requirements.

V

I have been remarking upon the power of ideas, as seen in every stage and phase of intellection. I found this power everywhere, promptly active and decisive, giving us effective and final discursion. So far, so good. This was part of my scheme. And I have maintained that we may designate this power, at our option, as emotion or desire, choice or will, etc., holding, nevertheless, that it is ever, and unchangeably, a vehemence inherent in our opinions or informations, yielding a volitional impulse, it may be, more intensely personal, when we have acquired the power to rate our conceptions in accordance with their bearing on our welfare.

And this leads me to explain that this more personal force of our thought is the discovery of rational impulses, called *emotions and desires.* For just as we remove the borders of ignorance, we discover our rational impulses, and throw off the yoke of blind propensities. But all the personal power you can put into emotions or desires is born of the thoughts or opinions which inspire them. This will appear as we proceed.

However, let us here contrast our blind impulses with our intelligent motors, emotions and desires. And in order to this, I call attention to the fact that we are being daily bred to an intelligent exercise of our capabilities upon the things of self and our surroundings. We may still have blind promptings, as aforetime. But our mind and moral powers keep up a tireless watch for their control, in the interest of a developing humanity which may retire, or qualify, or even nullify, any impulse not sanctioned by the now dominant personal (here emotional and desiderative) outlook.

I explain further. In other connections it was stated that, in its intercourse with things, mind brought home to itself only an idea or bare affirmation of things and their relations, etc., etc. Now

however, considering the careful study we are at
present making, of the real, psychological status
of the idea, this seems to be quite a beggarly im-
portation.   For it has been shown to be a *personal*
POWER, moving us to act, and faithfully releas-
ing the vehemence of our emotions and desires.
Whereas these latter, for their part, as faithfully
reflect the power of the informations involved in
conceiving and actualizing what we shall do.

Only a word more.   The question may be asked,
what shall we say of persons who are excessively
emotioned ?   I answer that, if any one apprehend
things or their impressions with a maximum of
emotion, we need only look for the cause of this
excess.   In every such case it will be seen that
some idea or information determines this emotional
overplus.   That is to say, some discovery of the
mind, resulting in choice, or personal preference,
asserts itself emotionally, to the point of redun-
dancy.   The motive power of emotions and desires is always with the intellections that inspire
them.   But I pass on to other considerations.

VI

In concluding this branch of our subject, I submit
that I have been able to establish some important
conclusions, the which I may presently summarize.
I need scarcely remind the reader that, in an act of
choice, the thinker has bestowed his final thought
and its power, upon what he is minded to do, and
that he does it in the selfsame instant by the
same power of thought put forward into his act

or deed, and that it is this last effort of thought which does the work, etc., etc. I have also expounded the offices of thought in other particulars. I have explained that it determines a condition of soul, for the infant, in virtue of which it becomes a *person*, competent to take a peculiar interest in itself and that world of alternatives which it propounds for choice and action. I have also shown that it has charge of our native propensities and vagrant passions, giving us true emotions and desires, for our rational impulsion. And I have likewise shown that these latter are our personal motors, and that they lean upon informations which reflect their every phase, from the most indolent conception to that irreversible one which has charge of the details of performance and conduct, maintaining ever that the operative stringency of our thoughts is our sole voluntary efficiency, and denying that there is such a thing as a will distinct from this.

And now pardon a word for myself, for I, too, have my share of thought and its power, and I can say that my whole life has been one unending, impetuous, uncrushable and consciously *thoughtful* (personal and responsible) irruption upon the kingdoms of matter and mind which allure me with their spoils, and repay me with discoveries which minister to the self-conscious little world of egoism I have built up of the force of my conceptions.

And yet, for colloquial reasons, one may be held to have a will characteristically indolent or energetic, resolute or vacillating, halting or determined, artless or astute, pliant or stubborn, etc., etc. But what is that, but the soft, or else severe intentness of the intellectual gaze, a phase or expression of the personal interest we all take in our own opinions, or convictions.

VII

If now I am correct in my exposition, why should we be the least concerned about our volitions (preferences or *choices*) being determined by motives or reasons ? Something must determine our choice, and if that is in the thought itself, then the determination is by a power of mental discursion, and therefore free and voluntary. I am overhauling the argument to make the points explicit and unmistakable. And therefore, I repeat that, if in this determination, we are employing an energy that is inseparable from, and an original element of, our thought, then we do but project the power of our decisive thought into what we do, and that, alone, is the energy we are in search of. And this domination of the stress of our thought or information, as expressed in our emotions or desires when consummated in choice of act or deed, — it is this dominant urgency of our thought, which implicates us with acts for which we are personally responsible. For thought makes us persons, and personally accountable, as well.

Now, if the power that goes into our acts is an element of the knowledge we acquire, it is in fact thought itself, grasping its objects by a power of its own. But now, if we take the position that this energy, so rational and so intimately ours, is in some way inscrutable to us, distinct from thought and its achievements, even then we might regard it in the light of an instrument, at our service, like, say, a finger whose activities are called forth by the power of thought and its distinctions. But whose distinctions, whose power? Plainly the man's own, by right of his active discovery of knowledge, and the moral (thoughtful) evaluations of both motives and conduct, — evaluations which make him personally accountable for his acts.

But again, some regard the will as a distinct actile power sufficient unto itself, as a voluntary cause set apart to do the work of volition, or choice. This theory has been abundantly adverted to in previous paragraphs. But now, without knowing exactly what is meant by such a will, allow me to observe that, even if we had a will, as a distinct volitional efficiency, we could never will ourselves discharged from the force of our reasons, without evicting our personal responsibility. For the very life of moral freedom hangs on the reasons that determine acts of choice. We can indeed act on either a good or bad reason, but we must have, at least, one of some kind, or not act at all. But whatever be our reasons, these fetch us choice, and not a power of will to do *anything*. The law for personal rectitude covers every act of choice, and this choice is simply our ultimate reason for doing something in preference to another something. For though free, we are bound by the enabling act which restricts us to our choice and conditions its exercise by a conception of the moral and other consequences involved.

But allow me to submit the so-called will to some further scrutiny.

We often say: The will determines actions. And this is correct, if we are referring to the will, as the personal preference of a competent thinker walking in the strength of some final conviction. Whatever may be our language colloquially, we can mean only that our actions are determined by what we think, when we act efficiently. And surely, until our thought turns unchangeably efficient in our acts, it may not have acquired the distinctive feature of an actile energy which fits it for the tasks and problems of life and acts. We see then, from these several points of view, that motives, reasons, informations, etc., determine conduct, determine personal preference and behavior, going forward into result as our conative energy resolutely final, and equally present and urgent in deeds, and the multiform elaborative processes of discursion.

The power of informations is always on hand, and always in season.

VIII

I propose now to see how this our power of reasons will deport itself when confronting still other and deeper problems of life.

I am taking it for granted that man acquires power in acquiring knowledge, and that this power determines all he does. And herein, he is free, and

so far *supernatural*, just as his Creator is supernatural. That he should make sure of what he
will do, and also feel bound by his moral appreciations and the sanctions of a divine law for personal
implication in, and responsibility for, all he does, —
this is an ordinance of God holding him bound by
his thoughts and acts. For, to be a moral agent,
the acts must have the power of knowledge. The
character of our reasons determines the character
of our acts. And this is the one unique power
(specialized, of course, according to the measure
and quality of our culture), which culminates in
deeds for which we are responsible. The conclusion
is irresistible that, when we act on reasons, we act
on their inherent force, but this force depends on
the personal interest we take in a self-conscious
condition of soul which we have made our own by
cultivating our intellectual powers. For now that
we have sought out knowledge, we do not lay it
on the shelf, but cleave to it and keep it in hand,
as part and parcel of ourself. And so when one
sees his own thoughts going over into conduct as
its cause, and dares to know of the divine sanctions
which bind a conscious actor to what he does, he
cannot escape personal responsibility for such a
venture, without the complete deformation of both
mind and morals. And, therefore, I insist that
every thought has a distinctive power of its own
which, on becoming causative, cries out: *Hoc est
agendum.* And this cry of peremptory command
goes with every variety of information, from the
most easy-going perception to moral constraint.

At first, to repeat, it may be but sparingly personal, the child not having, as yet, conceived any definite idea of its personal belongings, but it grows with the growth of our educed humanities.

It may proceed from some gentle idealism which suggests only indifference to action. But when it nestles in the practical honesties of a responsible soul, the fervor of this personal power will be immeasurably intensified.

And, permit me to remark, in passing, that the power which is begotten of all knowledge is in itself an element of irresistible attraction to man. Indeed, it is chiefly this thing of its power which impels us to search for, and so make use of, the constructive ideas of Omniscience placed within our reach. For, as before explained, He has spoken to our intelligence in all we see of matter and mind, and we amass all our knowledge by a most literal certification of some of His thoughts.

So too, after the manner of His mind, but within finite limits, we may put the power of our thoughts into the work of our hands, and this finite work of our hands will have place in our day as a new creation, giving forth ideas of cause and effect, subject and attribute, purpose, meaning, principle, etc., just as His works do, — and because all work proclaims knowledge. And therefore, do I maintain that, in all this thing of perception and conception, the human mind is an autonomy of rational capacities, equipped for the tasks of discursion and deeds. And, if it ever is to have this power, it is because of an original ordinance which fits it for achieving ideas — ideas which are born of the fiat of our discursive processes, starting from the rational centre in quest of the rational coördination of all things we affirm in the domains of matter and mind.

IX

Our long discussion must now close, and what I have hitherto written must be left in garrison, to conserve the positions gained, whilst, withal, it behooves me, for my part, to "pass over the river and rest in the shade."

I conclude with a brief summary of the points urged: The power of thought is always in hand, always in season, and always efficient. Its vigor is born with, and part and parcel of, its achievement. So also is its distinctive quality or individuality. If it be of the stupid kind, it is, so far forth, robbed of its normal rôle of action. Nevertheless, it would be a sheer monstrosity, if any information, however feeble, should be deficient in its proper vigor. The very soul of an idea is its individual vigor, be it strong, or be it feeble.

But what becomes of this power when we are engaged in a decisive act? It is, as before averred, promptly present, and, upon the touch of opportunity, moves into position, and passes like current gold.

But here I must be careful to get all the facts before me. Even the opportune moment for decisive action is a problem to be solved by an appreciation of the facts, and judgment on their evidential force. Moreover, even the force of our reasons is kept under control by the force of other reasons which determine conduct finally; for one may not go into acts for which he knows he will be personally responsible, until he is satisfied of the reasons which, from his then point of view, he can make free to act upon.

Hence, the latent stress of every thought that solves questions of business, duty, or personal responsibility, or even personal worthlessness, is never brought out, until we are convinced that we can act with required resolution, precision, and efficiency, in making the attack. And so it comes to this that mental and moral power is born of the force of our ideas, and the idea itself is simply a discursive achievement of one competent to report it. Wherefore, whenever such an one has acquired an idea, he has, *ipso facto*, acquired its actile force. And this force goes into what we do, as our voluntary efficiency, or the finalizing vehemence of our thought. And very doubtless, even from the first intellections of the child, an idea once acquired, becomes a personal fervor, emotional or desiderative, tingling with causative expectancy. For how could it maintain itself, even for an instant, out of all connection with the person who conceives and plans for its fulfilment, — of course very artlessly in the beginnings of infantile discursion? But thenceforward, every idea, from every source, becomes more and more a personal power, or voluntary impulsion, expressed in emotion, or desire, and ultimated in work, or conduct. And so, I conclude that every information, reached by attention and mental elaboration, has, in itself, a power which passes over into deeds or acts, as our personal and voluntary efficiency. Nay, more, it is an investment in mental and moral culture which is kept in store for the exigencies of future action and conduct — the acquisition of a first idea, with its peculiar power, helping on to a second, with its peculiar power, and so on, *ad infinitum*. And this power seats itself so firmly in what it accomplishes that you cannot even conceive of its inhibition *in loco*.

The reader can say whether there is any will, or need of any, conceived as distinctly separable from the inherent force of the reasons on which we act.

There is pluck and determination in an idea. It is born to rule. It asserts undivided sway over the empire of volition and morals. It forges its way to performance with a tenacity of purpose almost ferocious. It is ubiquitous. It is a pervading presence. It has stood every pressure from the beginning. It informs and empowers everything, from the minutest atoms to the "mills of the Gods." It is a law for a universe of entities. It is our personal and voluntary competency. It is salted with the salt of all our possibilities. It shapes our ends. It has charge of all our humanities. It spans the confines of time, space, and eternity. It is irrepressible, and cannot be ruled out. It has come to stay.